TEEN EDITION

FACING ★ YOUR ★ GIANTS

MAX LUCADO

ADAPTED BY MONICA HALL

MJF BOOKS
NEW YORK

Published by MJF Books
Fine Communications
322 Eighth Avenue
New York, NY 10001

Facing Your Giants
LC Control Number: 2012950965
ISBN-13: 978-1-60671-171-2
ISBN-10: 1-60671-171-7

Karen Hill, Administrative Editor for Max Lucado

This edition is published by MJF Books in arrangement with Thomas Nelson, Inc.

All Scripture quotations, unless otherwise indicated, are taken from The New King James Version, copyright © 1979, 1980, 1982, Thomas Nelson, Inc., Publishers.

Other Scripture references are from the following sources:
The American Standard Version (ASV). God's Word (God's Word) is a copyrighted work of God's Word to the Nations Bible Society. Quotations are used by permission. Copyright © 1995 by God's Word to the Nations Bible Society. All rights reserved. The Good News Bible: The Bible in Today's English Version (TEV), copyright © 1992 by the American Bible Society. The Message (MSG), copyright © 1993, 1994, 1995, 1996, 2000, 2001, 2002. Used by permission of NavPress Publishing Group. New American Standard Bible (NASB), copyright © 1960, 1977, 1995 by the Lockman Foundation. The New Century Version® (NCV), copyright © 2005 by Thomas Nelson, Inc. Used by permission. All rights reserved. The Holy Bible, New International Version (NIV), copyright © 1973, 1978, 1984, International Bible Society. Used by permission of Zondervan Bible Publishers. Holy Bible, New Living Translation (NLT), copyright © 1996. Used by permission of Tyndale House Publishers, Inc., Wheaton, Illinois 60189. All rights reserved. J. B. Phillips: The New Testament in Modern English, Revised Edition (PHILLIPS), copyright © J. B. Phillips 1958, 1960, 1972. Used by permission of Macmillan Publishing Co., Inc.

Interior art and layout by Kay Meadows

Printed in the United States of America.

MJF Books and the MJF colophon are trademarks of Fine Creative Media, Inc.

BG   10 9 8 7 6 5 4 3 2 1

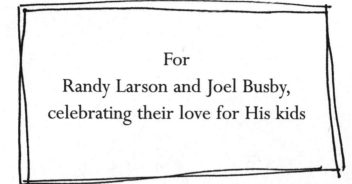

For
Randy Larson and Joel Busby,
celebrating their love for His kids

CONTENTS

Acknowledgments   viii
A Letter from Max Lucado   ix

1   Facing Your Giants   1

2   Silent Phones   16

3   Raging Sauls (and Other Catastrophes)   30

4   Grief-Givers   45

5   Barbaric Behavior   59

6   Slump Guns   71

7   Plopping Points   85

8   Unspeakable Grief   97

9   Blind Intersections   109

10   Strongholds   125

11   Tough Promises   138

12   Thin Air-ogance   155

13   Colossal Collapses   167

14   Dashed Hopes   178

15   Take Goliath Down!   188

Notes   198

ACKNOWLEDGMENTS

Grateful appreciation for the folks who made this book a reality: Monica Hall—your skill at writing for teens is unsurpassed. Beverly Phillips and June Ford—thanks for your careful editing. Mary Philippus and Dylan Connell—your keen insight into teens gives this book authenticity.

Thanks!

Dear Friend,

What giants are you facing?

The first day at a school?
Last place on the team?
A family member who doesn't understand you?
A friend who refuses to help you?

Giants. We all face them. But we don't have to face them alone. The same God who gave young David strength to face Goliath is willing to help you with yours.

Do yourself a favor. Spend some moments following the life of David through his decades of struggles. Sometimes he succeeded. Sometimes he failed. But each time he inspires us to face our giants by facing God first.

I hope you enjoy this special edition of *Facing Your Giants*. After all, giants come with life. But gratefully, so does God.

Max Lucado

Facing your Giants

Chapter 1

The slender, beardless boy kneels by the brook. Mud moistens his knees. Bubbling water cools his hand. Were he to notice, he could study his handsome features in the water. Hair the color of copper. Tanned, sanguine skin and eyes that steal the breath of Hebrew maidens. He searches not for his reflection, however, but for rocks. Stones. Smooth stones. The kind that stack neatly in a shepherd's pouch, rest flush against a shepherd's leather sling. Flat rocks that balance heavy in the palm and missile with comet-crashing force into the head of a lion, a bear, or, in this case, a giant.

Goliath stares down from the hillside. Only disbelief keeps him from laughing. He and his Philistine herd have rendered their half of the valley into a forest of spears; a growling, bloodthirsty gang of hoodlums boasting do-rags, BO, and barbed-wire tattoos.

Goliath towers above them all: nine feet nine inches tall in his stocking feet, wearing 125 pounds of armor and snarling like the main contender at the World Wrestling Federation championship. He wears a size 20 collar, a 10½ hat, and a 56-inch belt. His biceps burst and his thigh muscles ripple. His boasts belch through the canyon. "This day I defy the ranks of Israel! Give me a man and let us fight each other" (1 Samuel 17:10 NIV). *Who will go mano a mano conmigo? Give me your best shot.*

No Hebrew volunteers. Until today. Until David.

David just showed up this morning. He clocked out of sheep watching to deliver bread and cheese to his brothers on the battlefront. That's where David hears Goliath defying God, and that's when David makes his decision. Then he takes his staff in his hand, and he chooses for himself five smooth stones from the brook. He puts them in a shepherd's pouch that he has, and his sling is in his hand. And he draws near to the Philistine (17:40).[1]

◉ ◉ ◉

Connor. Margaret. Cody. Sarah. Kyle. If you asked the five of them now when they *first* heard the David-and-Goliath story, they probably couldn't tell you. In a Bible stories picture book? In Sunday school? In encouraging words from Mom or Dad about how *little* didn't necessarily mean powerless? Possibly. Probably. Who could say?

For them it was the story that mattered. From the very first time, and every time since, any mention of David-the-Giant-Slayer had their wide-eyed attention. Little guy. Big enemy. Amazing victory. What's *NOT* to like?!

But it wasn't until their fourth-grade summer, when a teenage whirlwind swept in to take over their vacation Bible school class, that they began to see how much more there was to this shepherd-boy giant-slayer who grew up to be a king.

"Hi, I'm Cassie. And have I got a story for you!"

The dozen rambunctious nine-year-olds in the class went mouse-quiet. From Cody . . . to Margaret . . . to Sarah . . . to Connor . . . to Kyle . . . and on through the class, glance met glance to send astonishment and speculation zipping around the room.

OH YEAH! Cassie?! *That* Cassie? Who else could it be? Yes, it is . . . Cassie Hamilton!

Cassie—whose flashing smile and copper-colored hair were impossible to miss.

Cassie—whose amusing chatter made it easy to pretend you didn't see that she had a—(Besides, it wasn't polite to stare.)

Cassie—who was something of an unlikely hero herself—was teaching *their* class!

THIS IS THEIR HERO?

This? . . . THIS is their hero?! Not at all impressed by David, Goliath scoffs at the kid, nicknames him Squirt. "Am I a dog, that you come to me with sticks?" (1 Samuel 17:43 NASB). Skinny, scrawny David. Bulky, brutish Goliath. The toothpick versus the

3

tornado. The minibike attacking the eighteen-wheeler. The toy poodle taking on the Rottweiler. What chance do you give David against his giant?

A better chance, maybe, than you give yourself against yours.

Your goliath doesn't carry sword or shield; he brandishes blades of discontent, anger, shame, or temptation. Your giant doesn't parade up and down the hills of Elah; he prances through your bedroom, your classroom, your mind. He brings expectations you can't meet, grades you can't make, people you can't please, forbidden things you can't resist, a family you can't escape, and a future you can't face.

You know well the roar of Goliath.

David faced one who foghorned his challenges morning and night. "For forty days, twice a day, morning and evening, the Philistine giant strutted in front of the Israelite army" (17:16 NLT). Yours does the same. First thought of the morning, last worry of the night; your goliath dominates your day and infuriates your joy.

How long has he stalked you? Goliath's family was an ancient foe of the Israelites. Joshua drove them out of the Promised Land three hundred years earlier. He destroyed everyone except the residents of three cities: Gaza, Gath, and Ashdod. Gath and Ashdod bred giants like Yosemite grows sequoias. Guess where Goliath was raised. See the "G" on his letter jacket? Gath High School. His ancestors were to Hebrews what pirates were to Her Majesty's navy.

Saul's soldiers saw Goliath and mumbled, "Not again. My dad fought his dad. My granddad fought his granddad."

4

You've groaned similar words. "I'm becoming a braggart just like my father." "My sister couldn't keep a friend, either. Why do I keep messing up? Is this ever going to stop?"

Goliath: the longstanding bully of the valley. Tougher than a two-dollar steak. More snarls than twin Dobermans. He awaits you in the morning, torments you at night. He stalked your ancestors and now looms over you. He blocks the sun and leaves you standing in the shadow of a doubt. "When Saul and his troops heard the Philistine's challenge, they were terrified and lost all hope" (17:11 MSG).

But what am I telling you? You know Goliath. You recognize his walk and wince at his talk. You've seen your godzilla; the question is, is he all you see? You know his voice, but is it all you hear? David saw and heard more.

◉ ◉ ◉

Cassie did, too. The flabbergasted nine-year-olds all knew Cassie's big story, but none in that long-ago vacation Bible school class had any idea how much *more* there was to discover about her—*and* their hero David. Cassie was well acquainted with a giant of her own, but first she had to get their attention where she wanted it—instead of where it was.

Cassie's smile swept the room like a searchlight. "I know," she said, "you were expecting Mrs. Martin. But she's broken her hip. And you've got me. But before we discuss David and the fine art of giant-slaying, let's get rid of the elephant in the room."

Elephant? Here? Where?!

Cassie chuckled as a dozen pairs of eyes scanned the room.

"Relax," she said, "no peanuts required. This *elephant* is just a figure of speech for something too big to ignore that everybody's afraid to talk about. Something like this."

Then Cassie bent down, rolled up the right leg of her jeans, and tapped a resounding *THUNK* on the metal-and-plastic contraption that replaced the flesh and bone of her leg from the knee down. "Go ahead," invited the eighteen-year-old former track star for whom everyone used to predict Olympic glory. "Take a look."

There was a long silence, which nobody wanted to break. Except, *of course*, Connor, who never could resist being the center of attention. "Wow! That is a seriously high-tech pros . . . pros . . ."

"Prosthesis," supplied Margaret with, as usual, the absolutely correct answer.

"Well, of *course*, Margaret," huffed Connor, reclaiming his place in the spotlight. "Everyone knows that's what you call it!"

Cassie smiled to herself at the look Margaret sent Connor over the rims of her glasses. "Actually," she told them, "I call it Liz."

"Your leg has a name? Why? And why Liz?" That was Cody, in hot pursuit of one of his favorite things—any mystery.

"Well," said Cassie, "I had to call it something, and *leg* didn't seem personal enough for something that makes me so much more than I was before."

More? What more? How more? Cassie smiled at her puzzled class. Now she had them!

DAVID

"Ah," she explained, "*this* kind of *more* is an extra *something* that can change *ordinary* into *special*. It can change you not just on the outside like my Liz, but on the inside like David's 'more'."

"Bible David?" asked Sarah, who always liked to keep the facts straight, which Kyle almost missed because he'd started wondering how much a missing leg would slow *him* down.

"That's right," came Cassie's answer. "When David went out to face Goliath, he had a lot more going for him than just five smooth stones and a lot of attitude. And it was that 'more' that made all the difference. That same kind of 'more' can make a difference for you, too."

"A secret weapon!" breathed an awe-struck Connor.

"Better than that," Cassie said. "A not-so-secret weapon that *anyone* can use . . . if they choose to."

YOUR CLUE TO THE "MORE"

You'll find your clue to the "more" that powered David in the first words he spoke, not just in the battle, but in the Bible. "David asked the men standing near him, 'What will be done for the man who kills this Philistine and removes this disgrace from Israel? Who is this uncircumcised Philistine that he should defy the armies of the living God?'" (1 Samuel 17:26 NIV).

David shows up discussing God. The soldiers mentioned nothing about him, the brothers never spoke his name, but David takes one step onto the stage and raises the subject of the living God. He does the same with King Saul:

7

no chitchat about the battle or questions about the odds. Just a God-birthed announcement: "The LORD, who delivered me from the paw of the lion and from the paw of the bear, He will deliver me from the hand of this Philistine" (17:37).

He continues the theme with Goliath. When the giant mocks David, the shepherd boy replies:

"You come against me with sword and spear and javelin, but I come against you in the name of the LORD Almighty, the God of the armies of Israel, whom you have defied. This day the LORD will hand you over to me, and I'll strike you down and cut off your head. Today I will give the carcasses of the Philistine army to the birds of the air and the beasts of the earth, and the whole world will know that there is a God in Israel. All those gathered here will know that it is not by sword or spear that the LORD saves; for the battle is the LORD's, and he will give all of you into our hands."—17:45–47 NIV

No one else discusses God. David discusses no one else *but* God.

A subplot appears in the story. More than "David vs. Goliath," this is "God-focus vs. giant-focus."

David sees what others don't and refuses to see what others do. All eyes, except David's, fall on the brutal, hate-breathing hulk. All compasses, except David's, are set on the polestar of the Philistine. All journals, but David's, describe day after day in the land of the Neanderthal. The people know his taunts, demands, size, and strut. They majored in Goliath.

8

David majored in God. He sees the giant, mind you; he just sees God more so. Look carefully at David's battle cry. "You come to me with a sword, with a spear, and with a javelin. But I come to you in the name of the LORD of hosts, the God of the armies of Israel" (17:45).

Note the plural noun—*armies* of Israel. Armies? The common observer sees only one army of Israel. Not David. He sees the Allies on D-day: platoons of angels and infantries of saints, the weapons of the wind and the forces of the earth. God could pellet the enemy with hail as he did for Moses, collapse walls as he did for Joshua, stir thunder as he did for Samuel.

David sees the armies of God. And because he does, "David [hurries and runs] toward the army to meet the Philistine" (17:48).[2]

David's brothers cover their eyes, both in fear and embarrassment. King Saul sighs as the young shepherd boy races to certain death. Goliath throws back his head in laughter, just enough to shift his helmet and expose a square inch of forehead. David spots the target and seizes the moment. The sound of his swirling sling is the only sound in the valley. *Ssshhhww. Ssshhhww. Ssshhhww.* The stone torpedoes into the skull, Goliath's eyes cross, and his legs buckle. He crumples to the ground and dies. David runs over and yanks Goliath's sword from its sheath, shish-kebabs the Philistine, and cuts off his head.

You might say that David knew how to get a *head* of his giant.

When was the last time you did the same? How long since you ran toward your challenge? Or did you log in to a chat room, fire up

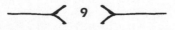

9

your iPod, or head for the mall instead? For a moment, a day, or a year, we feel safe, insulated, anesthetized. But then the challenges return and we hear Goliath again. Booming. Bombastic. Impossible to ignore.

◎ ◉ ◎

When you're only nine your personal monsters don't always come in giant economy-size like David's Goliath. But they're still pretty hard to ignore.

That midnight rustling in your closet . . . or under your bed! The kid who picks on you at school. Being so afraid of making a mistake that you never try *anything*. That icky nickname you can't shake. Monsters, every one of them. But they shrink right down once you realize that you never, ever have to face them alone!

"God will get you through it . . . whatever *it* is," Cassie told them. "He did it for David. He did it for me." Then, with an embarrassed shrug, "Of course, I didn't make it easy for him, especially in those first months after my accident. But once I decided to be 'David' and invited God in, he gave me the courage to face my giant."

The more Cassie's kids came to understand how David's power came from his trust in God to stand by him, the more they began to see the possibilities for themselves. Of course, as you grow, the bigger your giants grow, too. "The David Five"—as Connor, Margaret, Sarah, Cody, and Kyle had taken to calling themselves— would soon be facing their own giants.

But long after that vacation Bible school was over, the things they learned about David's amazing power source would see them through . . . as long as they never forgot that it was God who had their backs when giants showed up.

Just to make sure they *wouldn't* forget, Cassie had one more surprise up her sleeve. . . .

YOUR GIANT IS CALLING!

Next time your giant comes calling, try a different tactic. Rush your giant with a God-saturated soul. Amplify God and minimize Goliath. Download some of heaven's unsquashable resolve. *Giant of rebellion, you aren't entering my home! Giant of unkindness, it might take a lifetime, but you won't conquer me. Giant of anger, conceit, insecurity . . . you're going down.* How long since you loaded your slingshot and took a swing at your giant?

Too long? Hardly ever? Never? Then David is your model. God called him "a man after my own heart" (Acts 13:22 NIV). He gave the appellation to no one else. Not Abraham or Moses or Joseph. He called Paul an apostle, John his beloved, but neither was tagged "a man after my own heart."

One might read the rest of David's story and wonder what God saw in him. The fellow fell as often as he stood; stumbled as often as he conquered. He stared down Goliath, yet stared *at* Bathsheba; defied God-mockers in the valley, yet joined them in the wilderness. An Eagle Scout one day. Chumming with the Mafia the next. He could lead armies but couldn't manage a family. Raging David. Weeping David. Bloodthirsty. God-hungry.

A man after God's own heart? That God saw him as such gives hope to us all. David's life has little to offer the unstained saint. Straight-A souls find David's story disappointing. The rest of us find it reassuring. We ride the same roller coaster. We alternate between swan dives and belly flops, soufflés and burnt toast.

In David's good moments, no one was better. In his bad moments, could one be worse? The heart God loved was a checkered one.

We need David's story. Giants lurk in our neighborhoods, too. Rejection. Failure. Revenge. Remorse. We must face them. Yet we need not face them alone. Focus first, and foremost, on God. The times David did, giants fell. The days he didn't, David fell.

Test this theory with an open Bible. Read 1 Samuel 17 and make a list of the observations David made regarding Goliath.

I find only one statement to Saul about Goliath (17:36) and one to Goliath's face: "Who is this uncircumcised Philistine that he should defy the armies of the living God?" (17:26 NIV).

That's it. Two Goliath-related comments (tacky ones at that), and no questions. No inquiries about Goliath's skill, age, social standing, or IQ. David asks nothing about the weight of the spear, the size of the shield, or the meaning of the skull and crossbones tattooed on the giant's bicep. David gives no thought to the monster on the hill. Zilch. But he gives much thought to God. Read David's words again, this time underlining David's references to his Lord (17:27–49). You'll find, as I did, that—from the moment he sets eyes on Goliath until the battle is over—David mentions God nine times!

Nine references to the Lord. God-thoughts outnumber Goliath-thoughts nine to one. How does this ratio compare to yours? Do you ponder God's grace four times as much as you ponder your guilt? Is your list of blessings four times as long as your list of complaints? Is your mental file of hope four times as thick as your mental file of dread? Are you four times as likely to describe the strength of God as you are the demands of the day?

No? Then David is your man.

◉ ◉ ◉

The last day of that long-ago vacation Bible school was as surprising as the first. Only this time it wasn't Cassie's leg-named-Liz that had the students' eyes round with wonder. It was her special good-bye.

"Before you go, Giant Slayers," she told them, "here's a little something for you. Close your eyes and hold out your hands." Seeing Margaret's scrunched-up face, Cassie quickly added, "Nothing wiggly, I promise." Then with an intriguing *click* and *rattle*, a soft leather pouch dropped into each small hand.

Inside each sack were five smooth stones. "Like David's!" chorused the entire class.

"Well, not exactly like David's," Cassie said. "He had to settle for whatever was handy in the nearest stream. But I wanted yours to be as special as each of you."

And, indeed, they were. Each bag held five polished stones; but no two bags were alike. Cassie, perfectionist that she was, had spent hours that week at the rock and mineral show picking out exactly the perfect kinds of stones for every kid in class.

For Cody, who loved a mystery, the shifting golden fire of tiger's-eye. For restless, impatient Kyle, fiery carnelian. Deep purple amethyst for thoughtful Sarah. Bold red jasper for adventurous Connor. For supersmart Margaret, the subtle complexity of agate. And so on, through the class.

Tucked into each bag was a small scroll with a message from Cassie: "Keep these stones handy as a reminder of five powerful weapons that can bring down any giant: Past. Prayer. Priority. Passion. Persistence."

Then with a hug for each, she sent them on their way. "Remember," she said, "miracles do happen. And if you meet any giants, ask God for help . . . and expect to win!"

NO RED SEA OPENINGS

Some note the absence of miracles in David's story. No Red Sea openings, chariots flaming, or dead Lazarus walkings. No miracles.

But there is one. David is one. A rough-edged walking wonder of God who neon-lights this truth:

Focus on giants—you stumble.
Focus on God—your giants tumble.

Lift your eyes, Giant Slayer. The God who made a miracle out of David stands ready to make one out of you.

SILENT PHONES

CHAPTER 2

Other events of my sixth-grade year blur into fog. I don't remember my grades or family holiday plans. I can't tell you the name of the brown-haired girl I liked or the principal of the school. But that spring evening in 1967? Crystal clear.

I'm seated in my parents' bedroom. Dinner conversation floats down the hallway. We have guests, but I asked to leave the table. Mom has made pie, but I passed on dessert. Not sociable. No appetite. Who has time for chitchat or pastry at such a time?

I need to focus on the phone.

I'd expected the call before the meal. It hadn't come. I'd listened for the ring during the meal. It hadn't rung. Now I'm staring at the phone like a dog at a bone, hoping a Little League coach will tell me I've made his baseball team.

I'm sitting on the bed, my glove at my side. I can hear my buddies out playing in the street. I don't care. All that matters is the phone. I want it to ring.

It doesn't.

The guests leave. I help clean the dishes and finish my homework. Dad pats me on the back. Mom says kind words. Bedtime draws near. And the phone never rings. It sits in silence. Painful silence.

In the great scheme of things, not making a baseball team matters little. But twelve-year-olds can't see the great scheme of things, and it was a big deal. And all I could think about was what I would say when schoolmates asked which team had picked me.

You know the feeling. The phone didn't ring for you, either. When you auditioned for the part, tried out for the team, hoped for the invitation, tried to make up, or tried to get help . . . the call never came. You know the pain of no call. We all do.

We've coined phrases for the moment. "He was left holding the bag." She was left "standing at the altar." They were left "out in the cold." Or—my favorite—"he is out taking care of the sheep." Such was the case with David.

David's story begins not on the battlefield with Goliath but on the ancient hillsides of Israel as a silver-haired priest ambles down a narrow trail. A heifer lumbers behind him. Bethlehem lies before him. Anxiety brews within him. Farmers in their fields notice his presence. Those who know his face whisper his name. Those who hear the name turn to stare at his face.

"Samuel?" God's chosen priest. When Israel needed spiritual focus, Samuel provided it. When Israel wanted a king, Samuel anointed one . . . Saul.

The very name causes Samuel to groan. *Saul. Tall Saul. Strong Saul. The Israelites had wanted a king . . . so we have a king. They wanted a leader . . . so we have . . . a louse.* Samuel glances from side to side, fearful that he may have spoken aloud what he intended only to think.

No one hears him. He's safe . . . as safe as you can be during the reign of a king gone manic. Saul's heart is growing harder—his eyes even wilder. He isn't the king he used to be. In God's eyes, he isn't even king anymore. The Lord says to Samuel:

> "How long will you continue to feel sorry for Saul? I have rejected him as king of Israel. Fill your container with olive oil and go. I am sending you to Jesse who lives in Bethlehem, because I have chosen one of his sons to be king."—1 Samuel 16:1 NCV

And so Samuel walks the trail toward Bethlehem. His stomach churns and his thoughts race. It's hazardous to anoint a king when Israel already has one. Yet it's more hazardous to live with no leader in such explosive times.

◉ ◉ ◉

No one would call Kyle Perry a leader, which was stranger than strange; under the right circumstances Kyle could be very persuasive—even inspiring. Need an idea turned inside out or upside down? An intriguing question answered or asked? An exciting new possibility dragged kicking and screaming into the light of day? Kyle's your man! He's 100 percent *there* with you. Eyes intent, decisive gestures punctuating his enthusiastic words, Kyle would turn an everyday *interest* into an adventure. Until, that is, he was off and running in some new direction.

Long on enthusiasm, short on commitment, Kyle changed interests about as often, it seemed, as he changed his socks. And then he'd be off in hot pursuit of another interest—once again leaving behind him an unfinished project and another group of bewildered, disappointed, *almost* friends. Sure, he was great fun to be around for a little while, but his only long-term friends were The David Five—and he rarely saw them.

Shortly after the five had become friends in a fourth-grade vacation Bible school class, Kyle began building an impressive mineral collection around the teacher's gift of five polished stones. Soon the mineral collection was shelved next to a dozen other unfinished and never mastered projects. Next came karate, followed by chess, which gave way to computer games; then on to astronomy . . . woodcarving . . . roller-coaster design . . . math puzzles . . . meteorology . . . and about a bazillion

KIAI!

19

other things. But none of it was fun anymore. And he had no idea why.

As Kyle picked at his lunch in the noisy middle-school cafeteria, he knew something wasn't *right*. Oh, his busy mind was as sharp as ever. His urge to explore new territory still burned brightly. But lately there was that nagging feeling that there was something else—something important—he *should* be doing. *But what?! WHAT?!*

HISTORY CLASS HEROES

One thousand BC was a bad era for the ramshackle collection of tribes called Israel. Joshua and Moses were history-class heroes. Three centuries of spiritual winter had frozen people's faith. One writer described the days between Joshua and Samuel with these terse words: "In those days Israel had no king. Everyone did as he saw fit" (Judges 21:25 NIV). Corruption fueled disruption. Immorality sired brutality. The people had demanded a king—but rather than save the ship, Saul had nearly sunk it. The people's choice turned out to be a psychotic blunderer.

And then there were the Philistines: a warring, bloodthirsty, giant-breeding people who monopolized iron and blacksmithing. They were grizzlies; Hebrews were salmon. Philistines built cities; Hebrews huddled in tribes and tents. Philistines forged iron weapons; Hebrews fought with crude slings and arrows. Philistines thundered in flashing chariots; Hebrews retaliated with farm tools and knives. Why, in one battle the entire Hebrew army owned only two swords—one for Saul and one for his son, Jonathan (1 Samuel 13:22).

Corruption from within. Danger from without. Saul was weak. The nation, weaker. What should Samuel have done? What did God do? He did what no one imagined. He issued a surprise invitation for the nobody from No-wheresville.

He dispatched Samuel to Red Eye, Minnesota. Not really. He sent the priest to Sawgrass, Mississippi. No, not exactly. He gave Samuel a bus ticket to Muleshoe, Texas.

Okay, he didn't do that, either. But he might as well have. The Bethlehem of his day equaled the Red Eye, Sawgrass, or Muleshoe of ours: a sleepy village that time forgot, nestled in the foothills some six miles south of Jerusalem. Jesus would issue his first cry beneath Bethlehem's sky. But a thousand years before there was a babe in a manger, Samuel enters the village, pulling a heifer. His arrival turns the heads of the citizens. Prophets don't visit Bethlehem. Has he come to chastise someone or hide somewhere? Neither, the stoop-shouldered priest assures. He has come to sacrifice the animal to God and invites the elders and Jesse and his sons to join him.

Facing Your Giants

⊚ ⊚ ⊚

As sons go, Kyle was one of the good ones. It's just that his parents—like everyone else who crossed his path—had no idea what to make of Kyle. They loved him to pieces, this impulsive, multi-talented son of theirs. It was Kyle's lack of stick-to-it-iveness that troubled them so. *Such a waste of so many gifts!* When on earth would their enthusiastic bundle of contradictions catch on to the idea that it was as important to finish projects as to start them?

Lost in thought, Kyle nearly choked on his last bite of sandwich when his past arrived on quiet feet. One by one, four hands reached down and placed a neat row of four gleaming stones— jasper, agate, amethyst, tiger's-eye—on the cafeteria table.

Four smooth stones? Wait a minute . . . shouldn't there be a fif—? Oh yeah, that would be one of mine. With a wry smile, Kyle dug deep in a linty pocket to add the fifth stone—one of his own carnelian—to the array. *There . . . five smooth stones. Which could only mean—*

"Uh, . . . hi, guys," Kyle said as casually as he could. "What's up?"

"Glad you asked," said Connor.

"As a matter of fact . . ." added Margaret.

". . . there is something that's right up your alley. . . ." chimed in Sarah.

"We need an idea. A brilliant one!" finished Cody in a rush.

Connor. Margaret. Sarah. Cody. Four-fifths of The David Five had come to reclaim the one who'd wandered off. Half-embarrassed, half-delighted, Kyle grinned at these longtime friends. "Let me guess," he said. "This is about our eighth-grade service project. And you're the steering committee, right?"

Four nods confirmed it.

"Coming up with the right idea *could* take awhile," Kyle cautioned. "Perfect choices don't always come easily. Especially when there are so many interesting possibilities to consider."

No problem. Whatever it took to get it right. They'd wait.

PICK A KING

The scene has a dog-show feel to it. One at a time, Jesse's sons pass in review before God's priest. Samuel examines the boys one at a time like canines on leashes, more than once ready to give the blue ribbon, but each time God stops him.

Eliab, the oldest, seems the logical choice. Envision him as the village heart-throb: wavy haired, strong jawed, wearing tight jeans and a piano-keyboard smile. *This is the guy,* Samuel thinks.

"Wrong," God says.

Abinadab enters as brother and contestant number two. You'd think a fashion model had just walked in. Italian suit. Alligator-skin shoes. Jet-black, oiled-back hair. Want a classy king? Abinadab's your man.

God's not into classy. Samuel asks for brother

number three, Shamah. He's bookish, studious. Could use a charisma transplant, but bursting with brains. Has a degree from State University and his eyes on a postgraduate program in Egypt.

Samuel is impressed, but God isn't. He reminds the priest, "God does not see the same way people see. People look at the outside of a person, but the LORD looks at the heart" (1 Samuel 16:7 NCV).

Seven sons pass. Seven sons fail. The procession comes to a halt.

Samuel counts the siblings: one-two-three-four-five-six-seven. "Jesse, don't you have eight sons?" A similar question caused Cinderella's stepmother to squirm. Jesse likely did the same. "I still have the youngest son. He is out taking care of the sheep" (16:11 NCV).

The Hebrew name for "youngest son" is *haqqaton*. It implies more than age; it suggests rank. The haqqaton was more than the youngest brother; he was the *little* brother—the runt, the hobbit, the "bay-ay-ay-bee."

Sheep watching fits the family haqqaton. Put the boy where he can't cause trouble. Leave him with woolly heads and open skies.

And that's where we find David, in the pasture with the flock. Scripture dedicates sixty-six chapters to his story, more than anyone else in the Bible. The New Testament mentions his name fifty-nine times. He will establish and inhabit the world's most famous city, Jerusalem. The Son of God will be called the Son of David. The greatest psalms will flow from his pen. We'll call him king, warrior, minstrel, and giant killer. But today he's not even included in the family meeting; he's just a forgotten, down-on-his-luck kid, performing a menial task in a map-dot town.

YUCK ←

◉ ◉ ◉

Everyone knew Kyle was the perfect person to think of an idea for Oakdale Middle School's eighth-grade class project. This was a seriously big deal. Each year the eighth grade thought of, organized, and sponsored a yearlong community service project that would forever be their class legacy. Over the years, funds had been raised, gifts given, good deeds done—each more spectacular than the last.

It hadn't even taken Kyle long to decide to accept their offer. "Okay, guys, I'm in. Now all we need is the right idea."

Kyle found that idea in a news story about Hope Central, a struggling youth center that helps kids with problems.

....

"Hope Central? *That* place?" When he first floated the idea, the response wasn't exactly enthusiastic . . . until Kyle started talking.

By the time he'd finished, everyone in class could picture themselves trapped in that other kind of life: Being more used to anger than to love. Going to school hungry in dirty clothes. Struggling to get through day after day where everyone but you seemed to know what to do, what to say, how to act. Knowing everything about failure and nothing about success.

Yes, someone *should* do something, they agreed. But what? And what was spectacular about fixing up a shabby old building . . . or donating supplies . . . or . . . ?

"So, what would we do? Paint the place?" a doubtful someone asked.

"Much better than that," Kyle promised.

"Like what?" asked another skeptic. "Put on a fund-raiser, buy stuff for the center . . . give them things?"

"Not *things*," said Kyle. "What we give them is *ourselves!*"

And so *Talent Maximizer* was born. It was a simple idea really. Anybody who had a talent or special interest—and that was just about everyone in class—could use that gift at Hope Central.

Everyone agreed this would be the best eighth-grade project ever, until . . . their faculty sponsor appointed the project manager: Kyle Perry!

Kyle Perry, of *all* people. Sure, come up with the idea—but follow through, too? In that moment their enthusiasm shifted to thoughts of disaster. Kyle never finished anything.

For Kyle, *Talent Maximizer* became the "something else" he'd been looking for and the beginning of a more focused life. He made sure that once a week, every week, Oakdale Middle School eighth graders shared their blessings . . . and themselves. There were tutors in math, English, geography, and even one who started a team building parade floats. From

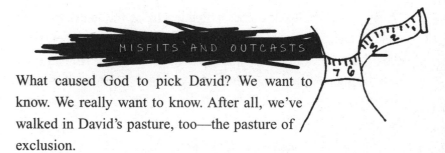

astronomy to zoology—and just about everything in between—there was somebody with a passion, a skill, a joy to pass along. Kids who had seen only limited opportunities were introduced to a world of possibility and hope for the future.

Though the other students hadn't shared his passion at first, Kyle never wavered. By the end of the year, the one-time class project was chosen to be a permanent service of not only the school's students but also the community. And Kyle? He could be found volunteering at Hope Central long after he graduated from college.

MISFITS AND OUTCASTS

What caused God to pick David? We want to know. We really want to know. After all, we've walked in David's pasture, too—the pasture of exclusion.

We weary of society's surface-level system, of being graded according to the inches of our waist, the color of our skin, the cost of our gear, the labels on our clothes, and the absence of pimples. Don't we get tired of such games?

The in-crowd chooses characteristics over character. The teacher picks pet students instead of prepared ones. Parents show off their favorite sons and leave their runts out in the field. Oh, the goliath of exclusion.

Are you sick of him? Then it's time to quit staring at him. Who cares what he, or they, thinks? What matters is what your Maker thinks. "The LORD does not see as man sees; for man looks at the outward appearance, but the LORD looks at the heart" (1 Samuel 16:7).

These words were written for the *haqqatons* of society, for misfits and outcasts. God uses them all.

Moses ran from justice, but God used him.

Jonah ran from God, but God used him.

Samson ran to the wrong woman, Jacob ran in circles, Ruth ran to a distant land, Elijah ran into the mountains, Sarah ran out of hope, Lot ran with the wrong crowd, but God used them all.

And David? God saw a teenage boy, serving him in the backwoods of Bethlehem, at the intersection of boredom and anonymity, and through the voice of a brother, God called: "David! Come in. Someone wants to see you." Human eyes saw a gangly teenager enter the house, smelling like sheep and looking like he needed a bath. Yet, "the LORD said, 'Arise, anoint him; for this is the one!'" (16:12).

God saw what no one else saw: a God-seeking heart. David, for all his foibles, sought God like a lark seeks the sunrise. He took after God's heart because he stayed after God's heart. In the end, that's all God wanted or needed . . . wants or needs. Others measure your waist size or your wallet. Not God. He examines hearts. When he finds one set on him, he calls it and claims it.

Silent Phones

....

By the way, remember how I waited for the phone to ring that night? It never did. But the doorbell did.

DING *DONG* Long after my hopes were gone and my glove was hung, the doorbell rang. It was the coach. He made it sound like I was a top choice and he thought an assistant had phoned me. Only later did I learn the truth. I was the last pick. And, save a call from my dad, I might have been left off the team.

But Dad called, and the coach came, and I was glad to play.

The story of young David assures us of this: Your Father knows your heart, and because he does, he has a place reserved just for you.

RAGING SAULS

(AND OTHER CATASTROPHES)

CHAPTER 3

Sharon checks her locker mirror . . . again. She studies the passing parade of students in the crowded hallway behind her, hoping there will be no angry Carla among them . . . again. Carla, and her group, has become a daily trial for Sharon. (Cross the queen bee, and the hive buzzes!)

Used to having whatever it was she wanted, Carla didn't like it at all when *her* Jason started paying attention to "a dumpy little nobody" like Sharon. Hateful looks and behind-the-back comments soon escalated to in-your-face tirades whenever and wherever Carla could catch Sharon alone. Now there were the nasty rumors. . . .

Sharon's not sure how much more of it she can take. So she checks her locker mirror . . . again.

Down the hall, around the corner, a quarterback named

Adam does some checking of his own. He peeks in the door of his coach's office, sees the empty chair, and sighs with relief. With any luck, the faculty meeting will run late, and he can leave a note proving he showed up, make his escape, and put off the tongue-lashing till another day.

When Coach Johnson's raging tantrums cost him his college coaching job, he decided to focus his energies on instilling the basics of the game in the kids who need it most. This fall, he brought his no-excuses attitude, exotic game plans—and short-fused temper—to Adam's high school.

Adam was here!

No one on the team had drawn a peaceful breath—or heard an encouraging word—since. Especially Adam—Coach's designated scapegoat for venting stress.

Sharon ducks her tormentor, Adam avoids his coach, and you? What ogres roam your world?

Controlling peers. The pit-bull math teacher. The self-appointed Popularity Patrol. The king who resolves to spear the shepherd boy to the wall.

That last one comes after David. Poor David. The Valley of Elah proved to be boot camp for the king's court. When Goliath lost his head, the Hebrews made David their hero. They threw him a ticker-tape parade and sang: "Saul has slain his thousands, and David his ten thousands" (1 Samuel 18:7).

Saul explodes like the Vesuvius volcano he is. Saul eyes David "from that day forward" (18:9).

31

 The king is already a troubled soul, prone to angry eruptions, mad enough to eat bees. David's popularity splashes gasoline on Saul's temper. "I will pin David to the wall!" (18:11).

Saul tries to kill Bethlehem's golden boy six different times. First, he invites David to marry his daughter Michal. Seems like a kind gesture, until you read the crude dowry Saul required. One hundred Philistine foreskins. *Surely one of the Philistines will kill David*, Saul hopes. They don't; David doubles the demand and returns with the proof (18:25–27).

Saul doesn't give up. He orders his servants and Jonathan to kill David, but they refuse (19:1). He tries with the spear another time, but  misses (19:10). Saul sends messengers to David's house to kill him, but his wife, Michal, lowers him through a window (19:11–12). David the roadrunner stays a step ahead of Saul the coyote.

Saul's anger puzzles David. What has he done, but good? He has brought musical healing to Saul's tortured spirit; hope to the enfeebled nation. He is the Abraham Lincoln of the Hebrew calamity, saving the republic and doing so modestly and honestly. He behaves "wisely in all his ways" (18:14). "All Israel and Judah loved David" (18:16). David behaves "more wisely than all the servants of Saul, so that his name became highly esteemed" (18:30).

Yet Mount Saul keeps erupting, rewarding David's deeds with flying spears and murder plots. We understand David's question to Jonathan: "What have I done? What is my iniquity, and what is my sin before your father, that he seeks my life?" (20:1).

Jonathan has no answer to give, for no answer exists. Who can explain the rage of a Saul?

Who knows why a parent abuses a child, a teacher belittles a student, a coach harangues instead of encouraging? But they do. Sauls still rage on our planet. Dictators torture, leaders disappoint, the strong and mighty control and cajole the vulnerable and innocent. Sauls still stalk Davids.

Sometimes when disaster comes calling, it's not a walking, talking "Saul" that looms on our doorstep. Instead, we find ourselves face-to-face with a circumstance—or event—that suddenly rips life-as-we-know-it to shreds. As it did for Cassie Hamilton.

It wasn't David's vengeful king racing the sleek red powerboat carelessly close to the water-skiers that August afternoon six years ago. But it might as well have been.

Cassie had noticed the reckless speeder as she skimmed along on her skis—noticed, but not worried. She had other fish to fry. Today was her last day at the lake this summer, and she intended to make the most of it!

Leaning her slender body out over the blur of water beneath her, Cassie edged her ski into another flawless turn. *Yes!* Now . . . *again*.

Then, like a toe stubbed on a curb, the tip of her ski dug into a choppy wave—and Cassie went flying. Up. Out. Down. It was an incredible fall. Then before her ski boat could race back to pick her up . . .

A roar and flash of red in the water above her.

A searing impact.

Then . . . nothing.

. . . .

Three days later, when Cassie woke up in the hospital, her world had changed forever.

"Welcome back, sweetheart . . ." chorused two trying-too-hard-to-be-cheerful voices.

"Mom? Dad? Wh . . . What happened?" *And why were there tears in their eyes?!*

Before that awful afternoon was over, she knew. It came back slowly at first: The joyful day at the lake. Her crashing fall into the path of the red speed-boat. The frantic, bloody race to the emergency room.

"Cass," said her dad gently, "now we're to the hard part, sweetheart."

And indeed they were. The spinning propeller blades of the boat that struck her had done too much damage to the bone, muscles, and tendons of Cassie's right leg. There'd been no choice but to amputate just below the knee.

Cassie the track star . . . Cassie the fleet-footed runner everyone expected to cheer on at the Olympics someday . . . was now just *half* the athlete she'd been three days ago.

"But . . . but how could this happen? And what do I do now?" What, indeed?

THE SAULS AND THE GIANTS

How does God respond to the Sauls—the giants—in our lives? Nuke the nemesis? We may want him to. He's been known to extract a few Herods or Pharaohs. How he will treat yours, I can't say. But how he will treat you, I can. He will send you a Jonathan.

God counters Saul's cruelty with Jonathan's loyalty. Jonathan could have been as jealous as Saul. As Saul's son, he stood to inherit the throne. A noble soldier himself, he was fighting Philistines while David was still feeding sheep.

Jonathan had reason to despise David, but he didn't. He was gracious. Gracious because the hand of the Master Weaver took his and David's hearts and stitched a seam between them. "The soul of Jonathan was knit to the soul of David, and Jonathan loved him as his own soul" (1 Samuel 18:1).

As if two hearts were two fabrics, God "needle-and-threaded" them together. So interwoven that when one moved, the other felt it. When one was stretched, the other knew it.

On the very day that David defeats Goliath, Jonathan pledges his loyalty.

> Then Jonathan and David made a covenant, because he loved him as his own soul. And Jonathan took off the robe that was on him and gave it to David, with his armor, even to his sword and his bow and his belt. —18:3–4

Jonathan replaces David's shepherd's garment with his own purple robe: the robe of a prince. He presents him with his sword. He effectively crowns young David. The heir to the throne surrenders his throne.

And then he protects David. When Jonathan hears the plots of Saul, he informs his new friend. When Saul comes after David, Jonathan hides him. He commonly issues warnings like this one: "My father Saul seeks to kill you. Therefore please be on your guard until morning, and stay in a secret place and hide" (19:2).

Jonathan gives David a promise, a wardrobe, and protection. "There is a friend who sticks closer than a brother" (Proverbs 18:24). David found such a friend in the son of Saul.

◉ ◉ ◉

"Hang in there, Cassie." "We're all praying for you." "You'll beat this, we know it."

Raging Sauls (and Other Catastrophes)

"Of course I will," Cassie assured her teammates, her confident smile pasted firmly in place. "Thanks for coming." Then, as the door closed behind the last of her visitors, she let her smile fade and turned her wheelchair to the hospital window. Cassie stared silently into the bright October afternoon.

Her friends had been great through the weeks since the accident. So had everyone else—the entire *town*, in fact! It seemed that everyone who knew, or knew of, Cassie and her amazing athletic talents wanted to be there for her as she struggled back from the injury that had claimed her leg.

And she appreciated it. Really, she did. But sometimes it was just all too . . . much. When you're sixteen, having your brilliant future ripped away in the blink of an eye isn't easy to deal with. Especially when everyone seemed to expect that she'd conquer this challenge, too, just as she'd always done in race after race.

Her champion's heart agreed. *Most* of the time. But then there were those other times—when her impatient spirit ran into obstacle after obstacle: Not-so-good news from her doctors. The frustrations of rehab. The struggle, like now, to see a future that could live up to the one she'd lost.

• •

Cassie jumped as the door behind her whooshed open. "Oops," said a husky little voice, "am I interrupting the party?"

37

"Party? Were my friends too nois—?" Cassie stared at the petite girl with the unruly mop of dark curls.

"Not *that* party," came the answer. "I meant the pity party."

What?!!

"Not that you're not entitled," continued her mystery guest, walking stiffly across the room to perch on the edge of Cassie's bed. "I've thrown a few of those myself. That's why I thought we should meet."

Unlike her visitor, Cassie was still at a loss for words. Who was this sprite with the incredible green eyes and more hair than anyone should be allowed?

The answer came with a friendly smile and an outstretched hand whose fingers cramped in toward the palm. "Hi, I'm Mia. Mia

Szabo. Szabo with a *z*," she added helpfully. "It's an Hungarian name. Probably even gypsy, according to my grandmother. She thinks that's where the violin comes in."

"Violin?" echoed a hopelessly confused Cassie.

Mia nodded, then raced on. "You see, I was a prodigy, too, just like you. Only my gift was music—the violin. For a while. Until the arthritis." Her smile dimmed for a moment. "And there went Juilliard . . . the concert stage . . . everything." She shrugged. "But that's another story."

"Arthritis?" Cassie was lost on page one of *this* story. Someone close to her own age with arthritis?!

"I know, it sounds weird," said Mia, "but it's not a disease reserved just for old folks. Trust me, I've got it." Then the beaming smile came back. "But enough about *me*; let's talk about you."

Cassie wasn't sure she wanted to. What was there to talk about?

Mia seemed to know. "You know, the usual: Confusion. Worry. Frustration. And anger—sometimes even with God?"

Cassie nodded. Yes, she did have her moments, and questions—especially the most troubling of all: *What* was God thinking to allow this?!

"Been there, done that," said Mia. "I've traveled this road—still on it in fact—and I know how hard it is. Especially when things don't go well and you feel like you're **ANGER** not only letting yourself down but disappointing everyone else, too." **WORRY**

Exactly!

"So," said Mia, off **CONFUSION** and running again, "I thought maybe you could use a friend who didn't expect you to be a wonder woman *all* the time. Someone who'd listen when you feel like grumbling, dust you off when you fall, cheer your victories . . . and give you a shove when you need it."

"A shove?" Cassie was still sorting through the flurry of ideas. Then her lips twitched as she suddenly flashed on a mental image of the irrepressible violinist nipping at the heels—okay, heel—of the one-legged runner. *Could be interesting. Might even be fun.*

"Just a *small* shove," Mia assured her. "And only when you need it. Deal?"

Now Cassie gave in to the smile that had been trying to escape, and held out her hand. "Deal."

Oh, to have a friend like David's Jonathan. A soul mate who protects you, who seeks nothing but your interest, wants nothing but your happiness. An ally who lets you be you. You feel safe with that person. No need to weigh thoughts or measure words. You know his or her faithful hand will sift the chaff from the grain, keep what matters, and, with a breath of kindness, blow the rest away. God gave David such a friend.

He gave you one as well. David found a companion in a prince of Israel; you can find a friend in the King of Israel, Jesus Christ. Has he not made a covenant with you? Among his final words were these: "I am with you always, even to the end of the age" (Matthew 28:20).

Has he not clothed you? He offers you "white garments, that you may be clothed, that the shame of your nakedness may not be revealed" (Revelation 3:18). Christ cloaks you with clothing suitable for heaven.

In fact, he outdoes Jonathan. He not only gives you his robe, he dons *your* rags. "God made him who had no sin to be sin for us, so that in him we might become the righteousness of God" (2 Corinthians 5:21 NIV).

Jesus dresses you. And, like Jonathan, he equips you. You are invited to "put on all of God's armor so that you will be able to stand firm against all strategies and tricks of the Devil" (Ephesians 6:11 NLT). From his armory he hands you the belt of truth, the body armor of righteousness, the shield of faith, and the sword of the Spirit, which is the Word of God (Ephesians 6:13–17).

Just as Jonathan protected David, Jesus vows to protect you. "I give them eternal life, and they will never perish. No one will snatch them away from me" (John 10:28 NLT).

You long for one true friend? You have one. And because you do, you have a choice. You can focus on your Saul or your Jonathan, ponder the malice of your monster or the kindness of your Christ.

BIG ?

◉ ◉ ◉

"Did you find the answer yet, Cass?" Mia asked as they left rehab together weeks later.

"Answer *to*?" Cassie prompted.

"THE QUESTION," Mia said patiently. "You know, the biggie."

Cassie did know. "*WHAT* was God thinking?!" they chorused together.

"Actually," said Mia, baiting her hook, "there might be an even bigger question."

"Bigger?" asked Cassie, still a step behind.

"Think about it," said Mia, intent on reeling in her fish. "Run over by a boat like you were, you could have been killed. But

THE ANSWER

you weren't. For some reason, God wasn't ready to take you then. Seems to me that he must have something else for you to do."

"Something else? But *what*?" huffed an indignant Cassie. "How am I supposed to know what God wants me to do?"

"Well, have you asked him?" Mia asked.

That stopped Cassie dead in her tracks. No, she hadn't. In fact, she hadn't been speaking much to God at all lately.

Mia had a thought about that, too. "Maybe you should."

In her rumpled hospital bed that night, Cassie closed her eyes and talked to God.

"Sorry I haven't been around for a while, Lord. But I think you know why. There are some things *I'd* like to know, too. Will you help me figure them out?"

All she had to do was ask. And once she did, she started seeing her "tragedy" in a whole new way.

What if instead of a problem, she was faced with an opportunity? What if her loss was really a chance to reach for, and claim, some wonderful new purpose God had in mind for her?

What that might be, she had no idea. Now. But she wasn't going to stop looking until she figured it out.

And she wouldn't have to do it alone. With God on her side, *all* things were possible!

(PROBLEM) + GOD= OPPORTUNITY

WALLOW IN THE SLUDGE

Major in your evil emperor, if you choose. Paint horns on his picture. Throw darts at her portrait. Make and memorize a list of everything the Spam-brain took: your childhood, your best friend, a parent, your spot on the team. Live a Saul-saturated life. Wallow in the sludge of pain. You'll feel better, won't you?

Or will you?

I spent too much of a high-school summer sludging through sludge. Oil field work is dirty enough as it is. But the dirtiest job of all? Shoveling silt out of empty oil tanks. The foreman  saved such jobs for the summer help. (Thanks, boss.) We donned gas masks, pried open the metal door, and waded into ankle-deep, contaminated mire. My mom burned my work clothes. The stink stuck.

Yours can do the same. Linger too long in the stench of your hurt, and you'll smell like the toxin you despise.

The better option? Hang out with your Jonathan. Bemoan Saul less, worship Christ more. Join with David as he announces:

> "The LORD lives! Blessed be my Rock! . . . It is God who avenges me, and subdues the peoples under me; He delivers me from my enemies. . . . You have delivered me from the violent man. Therefore I will give thanks to You, O LORD, among the Gentiles, and sing praises to Your name." —Psalm 18:46–49

43

Wander freely and daily through the gallery of his goodness. Catalog his kindnesses. Everything from sunsets to salvation— look what you have. Your Saul took much, but Christ gave you more! Let Jesus be the friend you need. Talk to him. Spare no detail. Disclose your fear and describe your dread.

Will your Saul disappear? Who knows? And, in a sense, does it matter? You just found a friend for life. What could be better than that?

GRIEF-GIVERS

CHAPTER 4

The most sacred symbol in Oklahoma City, Oklahoma, is a tree: a sprawling, shade-bearing, eighty-year-old American elm. Tourists drive from miles around to see her. People pose for pictures beneath her. Arborists carefully protect her. She adorns posters and letterheads. Other trees grow larger, fuller, even greener. But not one is equally cherished. The city treasures the tree not because of her appearance but because of her endurance.

She endured the Oklahoma City bombing.

Timothy McVeigh parked his death-laden truck only yards from her. His malice killed 168 people, wounded 850, destroyed the Alfred P. Murrah Federal Building, and buried the tree in rubble. No one expected it to survive. No one, in fact, gave any thought to the dusty, branch-stripped tree.

But then she began to bud.

Sprouts pressed through damaged bark; green leaves pushed away gray soot. Life resurrected from an acre of death. People noticed. The tree modeled the resilience the victims desired. So they gave the elm a name: the Survivor Tree.³

Timothy McVeighs still rock our worlds. They still inexcusably, inexplicably maim and scar us. We want to imitate the tree, survive the evil, rise above the ruin. But how?

David can give us some ideas. When Saul "McVeighs" his way into David's world, David dashes into the desert, where he finds refuge among the caves near the Dead Sea. Several hundred loyalists follow him. So does Saul. And in two dramatic desert scenes, David models how to give grace to the person who gives nothing but grief.

Scene one. Saul signals for his men to stop. They do. Three thousand soldiers cease their marching as their king dismounts and walks up the mountainside.

The region of En Gedi simmers in the brick-oven heat. Sunrays strike daggerlike on the soldiers' necks. Lizards lie behind rocks. Scorpions linger in the dirt. And snakes, like Saul, seek rest in the cave.

Saul enters the cave "to relieve himself. Now David and his men were hiding far back in the cave" (1 Samuel 24:3 NCV). With eyes dulled from the desert sun, the king fails to notice the silent figures who line the walls.

But don't you know they see him. As Saul heeds nature's call,

46

dozens of eyes widen. Their minds race and hands reach for daggers. One thrust of the blade will bring Saul's tyranny and their running to an end. But David signals for his men to hold back. He edges along the wall, unsheathes his knife, and cuts, not the flesh, but the robe of Saul. David then creeps back into the recesses of the cave.

David's men can't believe what their leader has done. Neither can David. Yet his feelings don't reflect theirs. They think he has done too little; he thinks he has done too much. Rather than gloat, he regrets.

> Later David felt guilty because he had cut off a corner of Saul's robe. He said to his men, "May the LORD keep me from doing such a thing to my master! Saul is the LORD'S appointed king. I should not do anything against him, because he is the LORD'S appointed king!" —24:5–6 NCV

Saul exits the cave, and David soon follows. David lifts the garment corner and, in so many words, shouts, "I could have killed you, but I didn't."

Saul looks up, stunned, and wonders aloud, "If a man finds his enemy, will he let him get away safely?" (24:19).

David will. More than once.

Gotcha!

Biting back a grin, Connor Ryan stretched his lanky body into a more comfortable position and settled oh-so-innocently into his seat. He was still savoring the sight of Jason's bike skidding into the south end of the school parking lot just as the Ridgefield team bus rumbled out the *north* exit to head for the inter-state—and the regional swim meet.

No one else on the team had seen Jason's too-late-to-matter arrival. But then again, they weren't looking for it; they'd shrugged and given up on him half an hour ago. Connor, on the other hand, was counting on it. The fake *TEAM MEMO* changing the departure time that he'd slipped into Jason's locker had done its job! As payback for the itching powder Jason had sprinkled lavishly in Connor's Speedo racers at practice last week, it was a stroke of genius.

The Connor/Jason score was even. Again. But probably not for long.

The rivalry between the two of them—and lately the not-always-funny pranks and paybacks—had evolved through the years. Most of it, to be honest, was Connor's doing.

Connor, grade-nine version, is still the same spotlight-craving show-off he was in fourth grade. Only more so. Older, yes, but far from wiser.

A talented athlete and dedicated risktaker, Connor's bold spirit is rarely deterred by the thought of consequences. One of his favorite locations is on the brink of disaster—teetering. And, boy, is he competitive! So is his longtime rival and—as Connor sees it—nemesis, Jason Grant.

Grief-Givers

Jason's athletic talents match Connor's, gift for gift, sport for sport: soccer . . . baseball . . . track . . . and now, swimming. Whenever Connor thought victory was *his*, there would be Jason. And vice versa. So closely matched are they that it would be impossible to say who is actually best. Not that it mattered—except to Connor.

For way too long, instead of teammate, comrade—even *possible* friend—when Connor looked at Jason he saw only one thing: the competition. When Connor's drive to always be best kicked in, common sense flew out the window—as it had today. Thanks to Connor, the Ridgefield bus was on the way to one of the biggest swim meets of the season with only *one* of its fastest swimmers on board.

And that's how things went from bad to worse. And not for the first time.

Not long after his life was spared in the cave, Saul, once again, is hunting David. David, once again, out-shrewds Saul. While the camp of the king sleeps, daredevil David and a soldier stealth their way through the ranks until they stand directly over the snoring body of the king. The soldier begs: "This is the moment! God has put your enemy in your grasp. Let me nail him to the ground with his spear. One hit will do it, believe me; I won't need a second!" (1 Samuel 26:8 MSG).

49

But David will not have it. Rather than take Saul's life, he takes Saul's spear and water jug and sneaks out of the camp. From a safe distance he awakens Saul and the soldiers with an announcement: "GOD put your life in my hands today, but I wasn't willing to lift a finger against GOD's anointed" (26:23 MSG).

Once again, David spares Saul's life.

Once again, David displays the God-saturated mind. Who dominates his thoughts? "May the LORD . . . the LORD delivered . . . the LORD's anointed . . . in the eyes of the LORD" (26:23–24).

Once again, we think about the purveyors of pain in our own lives. It's one thing to give grace to friends, but to give grace to those who give us grief? Could you? Given a few uninterrupted moments with the Darth Vader of your days, could you imitate David?

Perhaps you could. Some people seem graced with mercy glands. They secrete forgiveness, never harboring grudges or reciting their hurts. Others of us (most of us?) find it hard to forgive our Sauls.

We forgive the one-time offenders, mind you. We dismiss the ones who trouble us in small ways. But the Sauls who make our lives miserable?

Were that scoundrel to seek shade in your cave or lie sleeping at your feet . . . would you do what David did? Could you forgive the scum who hurt you?

Failure to do so could be fatal. "Resentment kills a fool, and envy slays the simple" (Job 5:2 NIV).

Vengeance fixes your attention at life's ugliest moments. Score-settling freezes your stare at cruel events in your past. Is this where you want to look? Will rehearsing and reliving your hurts make you a better person? By no means. It will destroy you.

Enemy destroyers need two graves. "It is foolish to harbor a grudge" (Ecclesiastes 7:9 TEV). An eye for an eye becomes a neck for a neck and a job for a job and a reputation for a reputation. When does it stop? It stops when one person imitates David's God-dominated mind.

◉ ◉ ◉

Swim meet: The blare of whistles, buzzers, and starting horns. Excited voices echoing off tile walls. The sharp tang of chlorine wafting through the air like perfume. And there in the middle of it all was Connor—NOT enjoying himself quite as much as he'd expected.

A disturbing thought had crept into Connor's mind midway through the morning races: *Maybe I did go too far this time!* All at once, the idea of Jason's reaction as he'd watched the team bus leave for regionals without him wasn't nearly as funny as it had been last night.

It hadn't worried Connor at all, when he arranged for Jason to miss the bus, that he was messing with his team's chances for victory

as well. In a sport where the difference between first and last place is measured in thousandths of a second, he and Jason were so perfectly matched that, with *either* of them in the race, Ridgefield could still claim the gold. In theory, that is.

Ridgefield's disappointing loss in the team relays—without Jason to anchor the final laps of the race, and Connor slowed by a sudden leg cramp—had settled the question once and for all. The ongoing Connor/Jason rivalry, and parade of pranks and paybacks, *had* escalated too far. And, oh, how Connor hated losing!

As he took his place on the racers' bench that afternoon to wait for the 800-meter race (he'd drawn Lane 1, his favorite!), Connor was determined to make things right. For himself *and* the team. It seemed to take forever to call the swimmers to their starting platforms.

Then . . . *at last!* . . . the buzz of the "ready" horn. One final deep breath, and Connor stood up. But his Speedos didn't! *What . . . ?*

"Gotcha!" said a familiar voice behind him.

Jason? Here? How?! And what did he—?

But those were all mysteries for later. For now, all Connor could do—Speedos firmly glued to the bench—was watch as Jason walked to the pool and took Connor's place on the starting platform. Jason took the medal, too. Until he was disqualified for not being properly entered in that race.

52

Grief-Givers

It was the locker-room scuffle at the end of the disastrous day that sealed their fate. Connor and Jason had, indeed, stepped too far over the line—and landed in very hot water!

"I've had it with you two prima donnas," Coach Parker fumed. "You may be good, but you ain't *that* good! For now, settle down. We'll settle everything else after we get home—including your futures on this team!"

And there they were, face-to-face with disaster. Or opportunity.

FACING GOD

David faced Saul the way he faced Goliath—by facing God more so. When the soldiers in the cave urged David to kill Saul, look who occupied David's thoughts: "The LORD forbid that I should do this thing to my master, the LORD's anointed, to stretch out my hand against him, seeing he is the anointed of the LORD" (1 Samuel 24:6).

In the second scene, during the nighttime campsite attack, David maintained his belief: "Who can stretch out his hand against the LORD's anointed, and be guiltless?" (26:9).

In these two scenes, I count six different occasions when David called Saul "the LORD's anointed." Can you think of another term David might have used? *Buzzkill* and *epoxy brain* come to mind. But not to David's. He saw not Saul the enemy, but Saul the

anointed. He refused to see his grief-giver as anything less than a child of God. David didn't applaud Saul's behavior; he just acknowledged Saul's proprietor—God. David filtered his view of Saul through the grid of heaven. The king still belonged to God, and that gave David hope.

Some years ago, a Rottweiler attacked our golden retriever puppy at a kennel. The worthless animal climbed out of its run and into Molly's and nearly killed her. My feelings toward that mutt were less than Davidic. I wrote a letter to the dog's owner, urging him to put the dog to sleep.

But when I showed the letter to the kennel owner, she begged me to reconsider. "What that dog did was horrible, but I'm still training him. I'm not finished with him yet."

God would say the same about the Rottweiler who attacked you. "What he did was unthinkable, unacceptable, inexcusable, but I'm not finished with him yet."

Your enemies still figure into God's plan. Their pulse is proof: God hasn't given up on them. They may be out of God's will, but not out of his reach. You honor God when you see them not as God's failures, but as God's projects.

Besides, who assigned us the task of vengeance? David understood this. From the mouth of the cave he declared, "May the LORD decide between you and me. May the LORD take revenge on you for what you did to me. However, I will not lay a hand on you. . . . The LORD must be the judge. He will decide" (24:12, 15 GOD'S WORD).

God occupies the only seat on the supreme court of heaven. He wears the robe and refuses to share the gavel. For this reason Paul wrote: "Don't insist on getting even; that's not for you to do. 'I'll do the judging,' says God. 'I'll take care of it'" (Romans 12:19 MSG).

Revenge removes God from the equation. Vigilantes displace and replace God. "I'm not sure you can handle this one, Lord. You may punish too little or too slowly. I'll take this matter into my hands, thank you."

Is this what you want to say? Jesus didn't. No one had a clearer sense of right and wrong than the perfect Son of God. Yet "when he suffered, he didn't make any threats but left everything to the one who judges fairly" (1 Peter 2:23 GOD'S WORD).

Only God assesses accurate judgments. We impose punishments too slight or severe. God dispenses perfect justice. Vengeance is his job. Leave your enemies in God's hands.

◉ ◉ ◉

No doubt about it, it's out of our hands now. Connor knew the consequences of the trouble he and Jason had brought on themselves—the loss of their places on the Ridgefield swim team. How to make amends for letting down their team, their school . . . *everyone!*

"Disgraceful behavior!" had been just the warmup of Coach Parker's lecture to Connor and Jason after the travesty at regionals. "What is it with you two? Don't you ever look before you leap?"

It was what Coach said next that still rang in Connor's mind three days later: "This 'eye for an eye' stuff never works out. Haven't you ever heard the part about 'turning the other cheek'?"

Funny, Connor had never thought of Coach Parker as a Bible-reading kind of guy.

For that matter, there were a lot of people who'd say the same thing about Connor. Though there had been a time . . . once.

With that thought, Connor leaped off his rumpled bed and rummaged for his long-forgotten Bible. He finally found it at the back of a dusty shelf—next to a small bag of five smooth stones.

....

Changes of heart rarely happen overnight, but as Connor began to read and remember, he was moving in the right direction.

"Forgive your enemies?" Well, actually Jason qualified as more of an occasional annoyance. *Or a work-in-progress . . . like me?* "Do unto others as you would have them do to you"? Speaking as someone who'd sure been "done to" at regionals, that made a lot of sense.

It *all* made sense, so much sense that Connor just had to jump right into doing something about . . . everything.

....

Connor put off the phone call until Friday. Overtures of peace weren't his best number, he thought as he toyed with the five shining stones. *Still, somebody has to make the first move. So why not me?* He put the stones down, picked up his cell, and dialed.

"Jason? Look, man, we're nose-to-nose with a giant-sized challenge. And I don't just mean the swim team thing. Seems to me that God still has a lot of work to do on *both* of us. Want to talk about it?"

He did. And the more Connor and Jason talked, the more they found to admire—even like—about each other. Could friendship be far behind?

ENEMIES IN GOD'S HANDS

When you leave your enemies in God's hands, you're not endorsing their misbehavior. You can hate what someone did without letting hatred consume you. Forgiveness is not excusing.

Nor is forgiveness pretending. David didn't gloss over or sidestep Saul's sin. He addressed it directly. He didn't avoid the issue, but he did avoid Saul. "Saul returned home, but David and his men went up to the stronghold" (1 Samuel 24:22 NIV).

Do the same. Give grace, but if need be, keep your distance. Forgiveness is not foolishness.

Forgiveness is, at its core, choosing to see your offender with different eyes. When some Moravian missionaries took the message of God to the Eskimos, the missionaries struggled to find a word in the native language for forgiveness. They finally landed on this cumbersome twenty-four-letter choice: *issumagijou-jungnainermik*. This formidable assembly of letters is literally translated, "not being able to think about it anymore."[4]

To forgive is to move on, to not think about the offense anymore. You don't excuse him, endorse her, or embrace them. You just route thoughts about them through heaven. You see your enemy as God's child and revenge as God's job.

By the way, how can we grace recipients do anything less? Dare we ask God for grace when we refuse to give it? This is a huge issue in Scripture. Jesus was tough on sinners who refused to forgive other sinners. Remember his story about the servant, freshly forgiven a debt of millions, who refused to forgive a debt equal to a few dollars? He stirred the wrath of God: "You evil servant! I forgave you that tremendous debt. . . . Shouldn't you have mercy . . . just as I had mercy on you?" (Matthew 18:32–33 NLT).

In the final sum, we give grace because we've been given grace. We survive because we imitate the Survivor Tree. We reach our roots beyond the bomb zone. We tap into moisture beyond the explosion. We dig deeper and deeper, until we draw moisture from the mercy of God.

We, like Saul, have been given grace.

We, like David, can freely give it.

BARBARIC BEHAVIOR

CHAPTER 5

Months of backbreaking labor, daily beatings, and slow starvation have taken their toll on a young Scottish soldier named Ernest Gordon, who during World War II had become a prisoner of war in Chungkai, Burma. At last, desperately ill and too weak to care, he awaits a lonely death on the filthy cot he shares with flies and bedbugs. His native Scotland seems forever away. Civility, even further.

The Allied soldiers behave like barbarians, stealing from one another, robbing dying colleagues, fighting for food scraps. Servers shortchange rations so they can have extra for themselves. The law of the jungle becomes the law of the camp.

Gordon is happy to bid it farewell. Death by disease trumps life in Chungkai. But then something wonderful happens. Two new prisoners, in whom hope still stirs, are transferred to the camp. Though also sick and frail, they heed a higher code. They share their meager meals and volunteer for extra work. They clean Gordon's ulcerated sores and massage his atrophied legs. They give him his first bath in six weeks. His strength slowly returns and, with it, his dignity.

Their goodness proves contagious, and Gordon contracts a case. He begins to treat the sick and share his rations. He even gives away his few belongings. Other soldiers do likewise. Over time, the tone of the camp softens and brightens. Sacrifice replaces selfishness. Soldiers hold worship services and Bible studies.

Twenty years later, when Gordon served as chaplain of Princeton University, he described the transformation with these words:

> Death was still with us—no doubt about that. But we were slowly being freed from its destructive grip. . . . Selfishness, hatred . . . and pride were all anti-life. Love . . . self-sacrifice . . . and faith, on the other hand, were the essence of life . . . gifts of God to men . . . Death no longer had the last word at Chungkai.[5]

Selfishness, hatred, and pride—you don't have to go to a POW camp to find them. A dormitory will do just fine. As will the boardroom of a corporation, a school playing field, or the backwoods of a county. The code of the jungle is alive and well. *Every man for himself. Get all you can and can all you get. Survival of the fittest.*

Does the code contaminate your world? Do personal possessive pronouns dominate the language of your circle? *My* career, *my* dreams, *my* stuff. I want things to go my way on *my* schedule. If so, you know how savage this giant can be. Yet every so often, a diamond glitters in the mud. A comrade shares, a soldier cares, or Abigail, stunning Abigail, stands on your trail.

◉ ◉ ◉

Backtrack the trail of some spectacular achievement and you might be surprised at where it all began. But that's the way life works, one thing leading to another—some of the most important of those things happening in ways that are quiet, ordinary, and unnoticed.

Sort of like Sam Mitchell, who was the kind of guy who just sort of blended into the background. It wasn't that he was actually ignored, but he rarely attracted major attention, either. He was just *there*. Doing what needed to be done. Keeping on keeping on. Actually, a lot of people did know who Sam was—the quiet, sensible kid you could always count on to keep his word, get the job done, do the right thing. His definition of "the right thing" started with the golden rule of treating others as you would want to be treated, and that included just about everything else that involved integrity, honor, and kindness—especially kindness.

THE RIGHT THING TO DO

If ever someone knew exactly the right thing to do—and did it—it was a woman named Abigail. She lived in the days of David in the land of the Philistines and was married to Nabal, whose name means "fool" in Hebrew. He lived up to the definition.

61

Think of him as the Saddam Hussein of the territory. He owned cattle and sheep and took pride in both. He kept his liquor cabinet full, his date life hot, and he motored around in a stretch limo. His  NBA seats were front row, his jet was a Lear, and he was prone to hop over to Vegas for a weekend of Texas Hold'em. Half a dozen line-backer-sized security guards followed him wherever he went.

Nabal needed the protection. He was churlish and ill-behaved—a real Calebbite dog. . . . He was so ill-natured that one could not speak to him (1 Samuel 25:3, 17).[6] He learned people skills in the local zoo. He never met a person he couldn't anger or a relationship he couldn't spoil. Nabal's world revolved around one person—Nabal. He owed nothing to anybody and laughed at the thought of sharing with anyone.

Especially David.

David played a Robin Hood role in the wilderness. He and his six hundred soldiers protected the farmers and shepherds from brigands and Bedouins. Israel had no highway patrol or police force, so David and his mighty men met a definite need in the countryside. They guarded with enough effectiveness to prompt one of Nabal's shepherds to say, "Night and day they were a wall around us all the time we were herding our sheep near them" (25:16 NIV).

 David and Nabal cohabited the same territory with the harmony of two bulls in the same pasture. Both strong and strong-headed. It was just a matter of time before they collided.

Trouble began to brew after the harvest. With sheep sheared and hay gathered, it was time to bake bread, roast lamb, and pour wine.

Barbaric Behavior

Take a break from the furrows and flocks and enjoy the fruit of the labor. As we pick up the story, Nabal's men are doing just that.

David hears of the gala and thinks his men deserve an invitation. After all, they've protected the man's crops and sheep, patrolled the hills, and secured the valleys. They deserve a bit of the bounty. David sends ten men to Nabal with this request: "We come at a happy time, so be kind to my young men. Please give anything you can find for them and for your son David" (25:8 NCV).

Boorish Nabal scoffs at the thought:

> "Who is David, and who is the son of Jesse? There are many servants nowadays who break away each one from his master. Shall I then take my bread and my water and my meat that I have killed for my shearers, and give it to men when I do not know where they are from?" —25:10–11

Nabal pretends he's never heard of David, lumping him in with runaway slaves and vagabonds. Such insolence infuriates the messengers, and they turn on their heels and hurry back to David with a full report.

David doesn't need to hear the news twice. He tells the men to form a posse. Or, more precisely, "Strap on your swords!" (25:13 MSG).

◉ ◉ ◉

If you need a bold knight to wield a sword of righteousness, quiet bespectacled Sam Mitchell isn't that guy. If, on the other hand, you

need someone whose gift for kindness helps smooth the rough edges of life, even moves a mountain or two now and then—Sam's your man.

You'd never guess it to look at him, but inside that quiet, unassuming exterior lurked a remarkable talent. For a guy whose glasses were usually crooked and in need of a good polishing, Sam had truly amazing vision. Or maybe it was his unique point of view.

Sam had the rare ability to see *both* sides of just about anything. Put him in the middle of a disagreement or conflict, and it wouldn't be long before Side A and Side B began to see how much closer together they were than they'd thought.

When Sam looked at people, he didn't see the differences . . . he saw the person inside the difference. There was room in Sam's life for *everyone*.

So when a group started hassling a frustrated Ramon Sanchez, Sam stepped forward. "What's wrong with you guys?" Sam demanded. "You don't look Native American, so *your* ancestors must have been immigrants, too, at one time!" Then, into the shamefaced silence, he added, "When was it for your family, Ramon? Three generations ago?"

"Four," said Ramon, a proud glint in his eye. "My great-grandfather came to America in 1923!"

It wasn't a big thing that Sam did that day—keeping peace and helping an out-of-place newcomer—just one small kindness.

But because Sam held out that welcoming hand, Ramon became more confident and ended up with a chance to show *his* abilities. And eventually Ramon and his flamenco-style guitar music transformed the school's all-too-predictable concert band with a hot new sound. Who'd have dreamed . . . ?

WILD WEST IN THE ANCIENT EAST

Furious at Nabal's insult, four hundred men mount up and take off. Eyes glare. Nostrils flare. Lips snarl. Testosterone flows. David and his troops thunder down on Nabal, the scoundrel, who obliviously drinks beer and eats barbecue with his buddies. The road rumbles as David grumbles, "May God do his worst to me if Nabal and every cur in his misbegotten brood aren't dead meat by morning!" (1 Samuel 25:22 MSG).

Hang on. It's the Wild West in the Ancient East.

Then, all of a sudden, beauty appears. A daisy lifts her head in the desert, a swan lands at the meat-packing plant, a whiff of perfume floats through the men's locker room. Abigail, the wife of Nabal, stands on the trail. Where her husband is brutish and mean, she is "intelligent and good-looking" (25:3 MSG).

Brains *and* beauty. Abigail puts both to work. When she learns of Nabal's crude response, she springs into action. With no word to her husband, she gathers gifts and races to intercept David. As David and his men descend a ravine, she takes her position, armed with "two hundred loaves of bread, two skins of wine, five sheep dressed

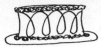

out and ready for cooking, a bushel of roasted grain, a hundred raisin cakes, and two hundred fig cakes . . . all loaded on some donkeys" (25:18 MSG).

....

Four hundred men rein in their rides. Some gape at the food; others gawk at the female. She's good lookin' with good cookin', a combination that stops any army. (Picture a neck-snapping blonde showing up at boot camp with a truck full of burgers and ice cream.)

Abigail's no fool. She knows the importance of the moment. She stands as the final barrier between her family and sure death. Falling at David's feet, she issues a plea worthy of a paragraph in Scripture. "On me, my lord, on me let this iniquity be! And please let your maidservant speak in your ears, and hear the words of your maidservant" (25:24).

She doesn't defend Nabal but agrees that he is a scoundrel. She begs not for justice but for forgiveness, accepting blame when she deserves none. She offers the gifts from her house and urges David to leave Nabal to God and avoid the dead weight of remorse.

Her words fall on David like July sun on ice. He melts.

"Blessed be GOD, the God of Israel. He sent you to meet me! . . . A close call! . . . If you had not come as quickly as you did, stopping me in my tracks, by morning there would have been nothing left of

Nabal but dead meat. . . . I've heard what you've said and I'll do what you've asked." —25:32–35 MSG

David returns to camp. Abigail returns to Nabal. She finds him too drunk for conversation, so she waits until the next morning to describe how close David came to camp and Nabal came to death. "Right then and there he had a heart attack and fell into a coma. About ten days later GOD finished him off and he died" (25:37–38 MSG).

When David learns of Nabal's death and Abigail's sudden availability, he thanks God for the first and takes advantage of the second. Unable to shake the memory of the pretty woman in the middle of the road, he proposes and she accepts. David gets a new wife, Abigail a new home, and we have a great principle: beauty can overcome barbarism.

Meekness saved the day that day. Abigail's gentleness reversed a river of anger. Humility has such power. Apologies can disarm arguments. Contrition can defuse rage. Olive branches do more good than battle-axes ever will. "Soft speech can crush strong opposition" (Proverbs 25:15 NLT).

@ @ @

Like ripples from a stone tossed into a pond, the relentless persistence of kindness *insists* on traveling on. So, of course, it didn't end with Ramon. When his chance came to pass along a little good, he took it.

Ramon had noticed that Kim Franks always knew everyone's lines in all the school plays, but she never auditioned.

"If you'd audition, you'd get a part," he told her.

"Me?! I'm terrified of being in front of an audience," she said.

But Ramon refused to give up. "What have you got to lose?"

What indeed? So Kim—who loved performing in front of her mirror—crossed her fingers, auditioned, and to her amazement was cast in a play! She loved it. And what's more—the audience loved her! By the next year, Kim had been cast in every school play and several community theater productions.

Once she'd opened the door to *possibility*, Kim held it open, too, for Suri Prabhakar. Suri, a shy little mouse of a girl, whose soft brown eyes and shining fall of blue-black hair cleverly disguised a mind like a steel trap. Suri had transferred to the school midterm, and Kim noticed Suri didn't make friends easily.

So Kim invited Suri to join her and some friends on a trip to a local planetarium and astronomy museum. Suri jumped at the opportunity to make friends, although an astronomy museum did sound a bit boring. (Wrong!)

Suri did make friends that day—but she also discovered a passion for the stars. She began spending endless hours gazing into star-drenched skies, imagining what it would be like to really go there. She joined astronomy groups and even attended a space camp for teens. Suri was reaching for the stars. . . .

. . . .

Years later, Sam Mitchell, lump in throat, would cheer the launch of the space mission that carried Suri Prabhakar to the stars. But he'd have no idea that *he* had anything to do with it—any more than he would ever know what grew from any of the small kindnesses he scattered into a not-always-kind world. He didn't need to know. All that mattered to Sam at any given moment was that it was the right thing to do.

POWER OF KINDNESS

Abigail teaches so much. The contagious power of kindness. The strength of a gentle heart. Her greatest lesson, however, is to take our eyes from her beauty and set them on someone else's. She lifts our thoughts from a rural trail to a Jerusalem cross. Abigail never knew Jesus. She lived a thousand years before his sacrifice. Nevertheless, her story prefigures his life.

Abigail placed herself between David and Nabal. Jesus placed himself between God and us. Abigail volunteered to be punished for Nabal's sins. Jesus allowed heaven to punish him for yours and mine. Abigail turned away the anger of David. Didn't Christ shield you from God's?

He is our "Mediator who can reconcile God and people. He is the man Christ Jesus. He gave his life to purchase freedom for everyone" (1 Timothy 2:5–6 NLT). Who is a mediator, but one who stands in between? And what did Christ do, but stand in between God's anger and our punishment? Christ intercepted the wrath of heaven.

Who does that? What kind of person would take the blame for something he didn't do?

When you find the adjective, attach it to Jesus. "GOD has piled all our sins, everything we've done wrong, on him, on him" (Isaiah 53:6 MSG). God treated his innocent Son like the guilty human race, his Holy One like a lying scoundrel, his Abigail like a Nabal.

Christ lived the life we could not live, took the punishment we could not take, to offer the hope we cannot resist. His sacrifice begs us to ask these questions: If he so loved us, can we not love one another? Having been forgiven, can we not forgive? Having feasted at the table of grace, can we not share a few crumbs? "My dear, dear friends, if God loved us like this, we certainly ought to love each other" (1 John 4:11 MSG).

Do you find your Nabal world hard to stomach? Then do what David did: stop staring at Nabal. Shift your gaze to Christ. Look more at the Mediator and less at the troublemakers. "Don't let evil get the best of you; get the best of evil by doing good" (Romans 12:21 MSG). One prisoner can change a camp. One Abigail can save a family. Be the beauty amid your beasts and see what happens.

SLUMP GUNS

CHAPTER 6

Goliath owns a slump gun: a custom-designed, twelve-zillion-meter, .338 magnum with a fluted barrel and a heart-seeking scope. It fires not bullets, but sadness. It takes not lives, but smiles. It inflicts not flesh wounds, but faith wounds.

Ever been hit?

If you can't find your beat, you have. If every turn becomes a detour, you have. Every step forward gets lost in two steps backward.

Relationships sour.
>Skies darken and billow.
>>Your nights defy the sunrise.
>>You've been slumped.

You feel like you're General Custer on your last stand.

David feels like it is his. Saul has been getting the best of David, leaving him sleeping in caves, lurking behind trees. Six hundred soldiers depend on David for leadership and provision. These six hundred men have wives and children. David has two wives of his own (all but guaranteeing tension in his own tent).

Running from a crazed king. Hiding in hills. Leading a ragtag group of soldiers. Feeding more than a thousand mouths.

The slump gun finds its mark. Listen to David: "One of these days I will be destroyed by the hand of Saul. The best thing I can do is to escape to the land of the Philistines. Then Saul will give up searching for me anywhere in Israel, and I will slip out of his hand" (1 Samuel 27:1 NIV).

No hope and, most of all, no God. David focuses on Saul. He hangs Saul's poster on his wall and replays his voice messages. David immerses himself in his fear until his fear takes over: "I will be destroyed" (27:1 NIV).

He knows better. On brighter days and in healthier moments, David modeled heaven's therapy for tough days. The first time he faced the Philistines in the wilderness, "David inquired of the LORD" (23:2). When he felt small against his enemy, "David inquired of the LORD" (23:4). When attacked by the Amalekites, "David inquired of the LORD" (30:8). Puzzled about what to do after the death of Saul, "David inquired of the LORD" (2 Samuel 2:1). When crowned as king and pursued by the Philistines, "David inquired of the LORD" (5:19). David kept God's number on speed dial.

Confused? David talked to God. Challenged? He talked to God. Afraid? He talked to God . . . most of the time. But not this time. On this occasion, David talks to himself. He doesn't even seek the counsel of his advisors. When Saul first lashed out, David turned to Samuel. As the attacks continued, David asked Jonathan for advice. When weaponless and breadless, he took refuge among the priests of Nob. In this case, however, David consults David.

Poor choice. Look at the advice he gives himself: "Now I will perish one day by the hand of Saul" (1 Samuel 27:1 NASB).

No you won't, David. Don't you remember the golden oil of Samuel on your face? God has anointed you. Don't you remember God's promise through Jonathan? "You shall be king over Israel" (23:17). Have you forgotten the assurance God gave you through Abigail? "The LORD will keep all his promises of good things for you. He will make you leader over Israel" (25:30 NCV). God has even assured your safety through Saul. "I know indeed that you shall surely be king" (24:20).

But in a wave of weariness, David hits the pause button on good thoughts, decides to get out of Dodge, and heads for Philistine country—and even bigger trouble.

◉ ◉ ◉

Years later when she could laugh about it all, Margaret Shelby still couldn't quite explain what it was that "made my common sense saddle up and ride off into the sunset." Sophomore slump? Mid-teen crisis? Brain slipped out of gear? Who knew!

"Whatever it was," she'd tell the teens she was mentoring, "Margaret Shelby Girl Genius came way close to sabotaging herself!"

Maybe it was the fun that everyone else seemed to be having that tenth-grade year that pushed her buttons so.

73

To be fair, all the extra work that went with honors classes didn't leave a lot of time for fun. *Still, I would like to be asked now and then.*

Maybe it was the way everyone—including Margaret—expected that she'd always be the one with the absolutely correct answer.

Maybe it was the feeling that the only thing people saw—or valued—in her was her blazing intelligence. *I do have other qualities, too, you know!*

How much reality was attached to any of Margaret's speculations was beside the point. The problem was, they wouldn't go away! For someone used to having all the answers, this relentless cycle of uncertainty was frustrating, depressing, . . . and more than a little annoying! Inside the giant dust bunny of gloom she'd spun for herself, Margaret was sure of one thing: she was pretty much fed up with being known as "the brain"!

Of course, there are advantages to being so smart. Her PSATs are off the chart. She already has her pick of colleges—with full scholarships included in the deal!

Unfortunately, Margaret was rarely at the top of anyone's invitation list for anything remotely resembling fun. It seemed to Margaret that no one ever looked past the brain to see what *else* she could bring to the party. And the more she thought about it, the more unfair it seemed. Yes, her extraordinary intelligence was a gift. But what good is a gift if it

makes you so *different* that you're always on the outside, looking in.

That was when Margaret decided that maybe being so *smart* wasn't at all the smart thing to be.

Slump Guns

PLAN TO ESCAPE

David's not-so-smart plan to escape Saul's wrath: Go where Saul *isn't* looking for him! Worth a try, right? So David leaves, and Saul calls  off the hunt. David defects into the hands of the enemy. He leads his men into the land of idols and false gods and pitches his tent in Goliath's backyard. He plops down in the pasture of Satan himself.

Initially, David feels relief. Saul gives up the chase. David's men can sleep with both eyes closed. Children can attend kindergarten, and the wives can unpack the suitcases. Hiding out with the enemy brings temporary relief.

Doesn't it always?

Unleash those hurtful words and you'll feel better—for a while. Break those inconvenient promises, and you'll relax—for a time.

Sample that forbidden fruit, and you'll be entertained— for a season.

But once the talons of temptation sink in, waves of guilt and remorse are sure to crash in. The loneliness of breaking up rushes in. "There's a way of life that looks harmless enough; look again—it leads straight to hell. Sure, those people appear to be having a good time, but all that laughter will end in heartbreak" (Proverbs 14:12–13 MSG).

That "amen" you just heard came from David on high. He can tell you. Listen to the third stanza of his song of the slump. In verse one, "he wore out." So, "he got out." And, in order to survive in the enemy camp, David sells out.

He strikes a deal with Achish, the king of Gath: "Give me a place in one of the cities in the country, that I may live there; for why should *your servant* live in the royal city with you?" (1 Samuel 27:5 NASB, emphasis Max's).

Note David's self-assigned title: the "servant" of the enemy king. The once-proud son of Israel and conqueror of Goliath lifts a toast to the foe of his family.

Achish welcomes the deal. He grants David a village, Ziklag, and asks only that David turn against his own people and kill them. As far as Achish knows, David does. But David actually raids the enemies of the Hebrews:

> Now David and his men went up and raided the Geshurites, the Girzites and the Amalekites. . . . Whenever David attacked an area, he did not leave a man or woman alive, but took sheep and cattle, donkeys and camels, and clothes. Then he returned to Achish.
> —27:8–9 NIV

Not David's finest hour. He lies to the Philistine king who gave him shelter and covers up his deceit with bloodshed. He continues this deception for sixteen months. From this season no psalms exist. His harp hangs silent. The slump mutes the minstrel. The music dies unborn.

◉ ◉ ◉

Tired of feeling cut off from the mainstream of school life—and desperately wanting to be appreciated for more than just her intelligence—Margaret had made up her mind to do whatever it took to fit in. And she set about it in typical Margaret fashion: Analyze the problem. Design the solution. Then act!

Maybe it's that old what-you-see-is-what-you-get thing. Ergo: Change the packaging! So she did.

She reconsidered her long-held belief that "two barrettes and a rubber band" were sufficient attention to the issue of hairstyling. But things were about to change. Margaret studied the latest fashion magazines with the zeal she once reserved for researching papers. Soon she had the latest hairstyle and had traded her oh-so-serious glasses for contact lenses.

She acquired an iPod and changed the ring tone on her cell from her beloved Mozart to something more hip and happening— though it jangled her nerves every time it jingled her number.

She experimented (briefly) with IM-ing, but the contracted spellings (weird) and grammar (none at all) disturbed her sense of order. Try as she would, Margaret simply could not *speak* shorthand!

She even considered—though somewhat hysterically when she pictured herself with pompoms— trying out for the cheerleading squad. *Get real, Margaret, even you don't believe that one!*

Signing up for every club, activity, and event she could get her eager hands on, Margaret threw priorities to the wind and herself into her pursuit of happiness with relentless determination. (*What good is an "inalienable right" if you don't use it?*)

Some of it worked. Some of it didn't. All of it was relatively harm-less—on the surface. It was with what happened next, on the inside, that things started getting pretty *iffy* for Margaret. When all of her look-at-me-I'm-just-like-you ploys were met with indiffer-ence, she decided it was time to cut deeper. If really fitting in meant outright ignoring her remarkable intellectual gifts, so be it.

Without a thought for the consequences, it wasn't long before things got completely out of whack! Less time spent on studying *did* leave more time for fun. Less time talking with God *did* leave more time to figure things out all by her maybe-not-as-smart-as-she-thought self.

SWITCHING SIDES

Things get worse for David before they get better.

The Philistines decide to attack King Saul. David and his men decide to switch sides and fight for their nation's enemies. They journey three days to the battlefield, get rejected, and travel three days home. "The Philistine officers said, . . . 'He's not going into battle with us. He'd switch sides in the middle of the fight!'" (1 Samuel 29:4 MSG).

David leads his unwanted men back to Ziklag, only to find the village burned to the ground. The Amalekites have destroyed it and kidnapped all the wives, sons, and daughters. When David and his men see the devastation, they weep and weep until they are "exhausted with weeping" (30:4 MSG).

Rejected by the Philistines. Pillaged by the Amalekites. No country to fight for. No family to come home to. Can matters grow worse? They can. Venom flares in the soldiers' eyes. David's men start looking for rocks. "The people in their bitterness said he should be stoned" (30:6 GOD'S WORD).

We have to wonder, is David regretting his decision? Longing for simpler days in the wilderness? The good ol' cave days? No Philistine rejection or Amalekite attacks there. His men loved him. His wives were with him.

Now, in the ruins of Ziklag, with men select- ing stones to throw at him—does he regret his prayerless choice to get out and sell out?

Slumps: the petri dish for bad decisions, the incu- bator for wrong turns, the assembly line of regretful moves. How we handle our tough times stays with us for a long time.

How do you handle yours? When hope takes the last train and joy is nothing but the name of the girl down the street . . . when you are tired of trying, tired of forgiving, tired of hard weeks or hardheaded people, how do you manage your dark days?

With eating or shopping binges? Turning off your conscience for an hour, a day, a month to check out those "forbidden" things you've been warned about? Doing your best to make everyone around you as mis- erable as you are? Many opt for such treatments. So

PAIN REMOVER

many, in fact, that we assume they reenergize the sad life. But do they? No one denies that they will help for a while, but over the long haul? They numb the pain, but do they remove it?

Or are we like the sheep on the Turkish cliff? Who knows why the first one jumped over the edge. Even more bizarre are the fifteen hundred others who followed, each leaping off the same overhang. The first 450 animals died. The thousand that followed survived only because the pile of corpses cushioned their fall.[7]

We, like the sheep, follow each other over the edge, falling into bad situations and making bad decisions.

Is there a solution? Indeed there is. Doing right what David did wrong.

He failed to pray. Do the opposite: *Be quick to pray*. Stop talking to yourself. Talk to Christ, who invites. "Are you tired? Worn out? Burned out on religion? Come to me. Get away with me and you'll recover your life. I'll show you how to take a real rest" (Matthew 11:28 MSG).

God, who is never downcast, never tires of your down days.

David neglected good advice. Learn from his mistake. Next time you lack the will to go on, *seek healthy counsel*.

You won't want to. Slumping people love slumping people. Hurting people hang with hurting people. We love those who commiserate and avoid those who correct. Yet correction and direction are what we need.

Slump Guns

⦿ ⦿ ⦿

Running as fast as she could in the wrong direction, it wasn't long before Margaret found herself in some very strange territory.

The girl who had always had all the answers now found herself not sure of *anything*. The confident intelligence that had always approached even the toughest challenges with absolute certainty was now second-guessing itself at every turn. The quick mind that could effortlessly assemble chaos into flawless order now found itself . . . *dithering*. Even the fun wasn't *fun*.

Margaret's master plan for fitting in had gone seriously awry. It had started out all right. The reaction to her initial change-of-image makeover had ranged from raised eyebrows to approving

smiles. It was her next step—putting the gifts of her extraordinary intelligence on the shelf—that stunned everyone.

Her parents couldn't figure out how she had gone—almost overnight—from studying "too much" to never cracking a book at all. Her teachers, who knew genius when they saw it, just shook their heads and sighed. Her classmates, who'd relied on the tutoring she'd always been so generous with, felt cast adrift.

And Margaret? Well, *she* was the most distressed, discouraged, and discombobulated of all. Being "just like everyone else" wasn't quite as enjoyable as she'd expected. She *actually missed* thinking. *Restless* and *cranky* weren't exactly the change of persona she'd had in mind. Worst of all was the feeling that she'd lost a critical connection to something important. And Margaret did know exactly what *that* was!

When she'd stopped talking to God—which she'd always done a lot more of than anyone would have guessed—she'd also cut off her power source. *I wonder if he misses me as much as I miss him?* she thought wistfully.

By the time *Wait a minute, what's going on here?* occurred to anyone—including Margaret herself—a lot of damage had been done. The always-perfect grades she'd intended to let slide just a little had taken a nosedive. She was on the verge of being dropped from the honors program. And an amazing gift was being shamefully wasted.

If it hadn't been for a perceptive guidance counselor who'd once gone pretty far down that same path herself, who knows how long Margaret might have been stuck on that road to nowhere she'd detoured onto. But Marjorie Norris had her ways—unconventional, maybe, but effective.

"Oh no!" said Margaret midway through their marathon session. "I got it completely backward! People hadn't been shutting me out; they'd been honoring my unintentional 'leave me alone' signals!"

Ms. Norris nodded. "Intense concentration can do that sometimes. Sort of like a giant 'Do Not Disturb' sign."

"So how do I fix things?"

"You're a smart girl, Margaret. You'll figure it out."

And she did. She also knew exactly how to start.

It's Margaret, God. Sorry it's been so long since our last talk.

82

HEALTHY COUNSEL

I discovered the importance of healthy counsel in a half-ironman triathlon. After the 1.2-mile swim and the 56-mile bike ride, I didn't have much energy left for the 13.1-mile run. Neither did the fellow jogging next to me. I asked him how he was doing and soon regretted posing the question.

"This stinks. This race is the dumbest decision I've ever made." He had more complaints than a taxpayer to the IRS. My response to him? "Good-bye." I knew if I listened too long, I'd start agreeing with him.

I caught up with a sixty-six-year-old grandmother. Her tone was just the opposite. "You'll finish this," she encouraged. "It's hot, but at least it's not raining. One step at a time. . . . Don't forget to hydrate. . . . Stay in there." I ran next to her until my heart was lifted and legs were aching. I finally had to slow down. "No problem," she waved as she kept on going.

Which of the two describes the counsel you seek? "Refuse good advice and watch your plans fail; take good counsel and watch them succeed" (Proverbs 15:22 MSG).

Be quick to pray, seek healthy counsel, and don't give up.

Don't make the mistake of Florence Chadwick. In 1952 she attempted to swim the chilly ocean waters between Catalina Island and the California shore. She swam through foggy weather and choppy seas for fifteen hours. Her muscles began to cramp, and her resolve weakened. She begged to be taken out of the water, but her mother, riding in a boat alongside, urged her not to give up. She kept trying, but grew exhausted and stopped swimming. Aids lifted her out of the water and into the boat. They paddled a few more minutes, the mist broke, and she discovered that the shore was less than a mile away. "All I could see was the fog," she explained at the news conference. "If I could have seen the shore, I think I would have made it."[8]

Take a long look at the shore that awaits you. Don't be fooled by the fog of the slump. The finish may be only strokes away. God may be, at this moment, lifting his hand to signal Gabriel to grab the trumpet. Angels may be assembling, saints gathering, demons trembling. Stay at it! Stay in the water. Stay in the race. Stay in the fight. Give grace, one more time. Be generous, one more time. Share one more blessing, encourage one more soul, swim one more stroke.

David did. Right there in the smoldering ruins of Ziklag he found strength. After sixteen months in Gath. After the Philistine rejection, the Amalekite attack, and the insurrection by his men, he remembered what to do. "David found strength in the LORD his God" (1 Samuel 30:6 NIV).

It's good to have you back, David. We missed you while you were away.

PLOPPING POINTS

CHAPTER 7

I recently saw a woman walking a dog on a leash. Change that, I saw a woman *pulling* a dog *with* a leash. The day was hot, brutally. The dog had stopped, totally. He'd plopped, belly down, in wet grass, swapping blistering pavement for a cool lawn.

The woman tugged and tugged. She'd have had more success pulling an eighteen-wheeler.

The dog's get-up-and-go had got-up-and-gone, so down he went.

He's not the last to do so. Have you ever reached your "plopping point"?

Blame it on your teacher. "Sorry, guys, this class has *one more* term paper to go."

Your coach. "Until we start winning, there'll be *one more* practice each week—on Saturday."

Your parents. "I've got *one more* chore for you to do."

Your friend. "I just need *one more* favor."

The problem? You've handled, tolerated, done, forgiven, and taken until you don't have one more *one more* in you. You are one tired puppy. So down you plop. *Who cares what the neighbors think? Who cares what the Master thinks? Let them yank the leash all they want, I ain't taking one more step.*

But unlike the dog, you don't plop in the grass. If you are like David's men, you plop down at Brook Besor.

Don't feel bad if you've never heard of the place. Most haven't, but more need to. The Brook Besor story deserves shelf space in the library of the worn-out. It speaks tender words to the tired heart.

◉ ◉ ◉

Reliable, energetic, superorganized Sarah Adams was . . . tired. Not just catch-a-nap tired. Not even sleep-for-a-week tired. Sarah was beyond-weary–to-the-core–FED-UP *tired* of what was her once-cherished role as "The Responsible One"!

Everyone counts on Sarah: Friends. Teachers. Parents (especially her own).

The irony of it was that Sarah had chosen that role for herself. No one forced it on her. Lending a hand . . . taking up the slack . . . saving the day . . . was as natural to Sarah as breathing.

Like many firstborns, Sarah seemed to have arrived on the planet with a built-in sense of responsibility. God had also gifted her with a

Plopping Points

warm heart and generous spirit. All of which worked out beautifully for everyone: her parents, who both had demanding jobs; three younger sisters, who thought Big Sis Sarah was the coolest thing ever; and just about anyone else who crossed her path.

"Sarah will take care of it" might have started as a family motto, but it tagged right along with her into the wider world. Mostly she

didn't mind. In fact, she'd thrived on being every-one's go-to problem-solver all through middle school.

Who would have dreamed that her first year of high school would bring it all crashing down? When Sarah carried on as usual—obligingly taking on every job, project, and responsibility that came her way—it didn't take long for things to get completely out of hand.

Before she knew it, Sarah was spending so much time on everything *but* Sarah that there seemed to be no *Sarah* left at all.

....

"This is NOT working. *I'm* not working, Phoebe!" Sarah informed the small Siamese cat curled in her lap. "Maybe it's time I reinvented myself. What do you think?"

Phoebe did what cats do best: looked inscrutable.

"Never mind," said Sarah, stroking Phoebe's velvet ear, "I'll figure it out."

She wasn't sure at first who the new Sarah should be. But there'd be one. And when that *new, improved*

Sarah emerged from the ruins of worn-out, old Sarah . . . *Look out, world, here I come!*

BROOK BESOR

The story of Brook Besor emerges from the ruins of Ziklag. David and his six hundred soldiers return from the Philistine warfront to find utter devastation. A raiding band of Amalekites had swept down on the village, looted it, and taken the women and children hostage. The sorrow of the men mutates into anger, not against the Amalekites, but against David. After all, hadn't he led them into battle? Hadn't he left the women and children unprotected? Isn't he to blame? Then he needs to die. So they start grabbing stones.

What else is new? David is growing used to such treatment. His family ignored him. Saul raged against him. And now David's army, which, if you remember, sought him out, not vice versa, has turned against him. David is a psycho in the making, rejected by every significant circle in his life. This could be his worst hour.

But he made it one of his best.

While six hundred men stoke their anger, David seeks his God. "But David strengthened himself in the LORD his God" (1 Samuel 30:6).

How essential that we learn to do the same. Support systems don't always support. Friends aren't always friendly. Parents don't always understand. When no one can help, we have to do what David did. He turned to God.

"Shall I go after these raiders? Can I catch them?"

"Go after them! Yes, you'll catch them! Yes, you'll make the rescue!" (30:8 MSG).

(I used to believe only saints could talk with God like this. I'm beginning to think God will talk with anyone in such a fashion and saints are the ones who take him up on his offer.)

Freshly commissioned, David redirects the men's anger toward the enemy. They set out in pursuit of the Amalekites. David keeps the men's weariness in mind. They still bear the trail dust of a long campaign and haven't entirely extinguished their anger at David. They don't know the Amalekites' hideout, and, if not for the sake of their loved ones, they might have given up.

Indeed, two hundred do. The army reaches a brook called Besor, and they dismount. Soldiers wade in the creek and splash water on their faces, sink tired toes into cool mud, and stretch out on the grass. Hearing the command to move on, two hundred choose to rest. "You go on without us," they say.

How tired does a person have to be to abandon the hunt for his own family?

Churches and youth ministries have their share of such folks. Good people. Godly people. Only hours, months, or years ago they marched with deep resolve. But now they're exhausted.

So beat up and worn down that they can't summon the strength to save their own flesh and blood. Disappointment has sucked their oxygen. Or maybe it was a deflating string of defeats. Family problems can leave you at the brook. Wrong choices can as well. Whatever the reason, the church—the world—has its share of

Tch! Tch! Tch! people who just sit and rest.

So what do we do with the Brook Besor people? Berate them? Shame them? Give them a rest, but measure the minutes? Or do we do what David did? David let them stay.

....

Well, I certainly can't stay in my room forever. So I'd better get on with it!

Once Sarah called a halt to her frantic pace to take some time for herself, she was faced with a *new* quandary.

Revolutions don't just shake up the status quo; they also, though it's seldom expected, shake up the rebel, too. Sooner or later comes the big question: *NOW* what?! Sarah was no exception.

First, of course, she had to get through the initial fallout when her usual yes to just about any request became a series of tactful, but firm, no's. Jaws dropped, eyebrows rose, hopes fell. What?! Their usually dependable workhorse was off duty . . . clocked out . . . taking a rest?!

Sarah's parents were about the only ones who seemed to think it was a good idea.

Plopping Points

"'Bout time you gave yourself a break, sweetie. Goodness knows you've earned it. Have fun."

It *was* fun. At first.

She finally had time for the books she'd always been curious about. Yoga class turned out to be . . . interesting; figure skating  a lot trickier than she'd expected; but the piano lessons were everything she'd hoped for—though it would take time. Then there was the mall. Oh, the mall! Who'd have dreamed there were so many fascinating possibilities in one place—all calling her name. After all, shouldn't the new Sarah be different on the outside, too? At least a *little*?

So one memorable day, Sarah plunged into the mall in search of a new look—and with her usual thoroughness, she overdid it. The new, improved Sarah was a shock to everyone—including Sarah. The clothes. The hair. The attitude. The tattoo?! (Small, but still a tattoo.) Her little sisters giggled. Her dad's lips twitched. Her mom sighed. Even her cat seemed bewildered.

"What do you think, Phoebe? Are the pink streaks a little much?" asked Sarah, fingering the spiky crop that had once been a shining brown ponytail. The little Siamese sneezed, tucked her nose under her tail, and went to sleep.

"You're right," said Sarah glumly, with a final frown for the mirror. "I don't like it, either." *What have I done?* (And it wasn't just her hair she meant.) *And where do I go from HERE?!*

RESUMING THE CHASE

David and the remaining four hundred fighters resume the chase. They plunge deeper and deeper into the desert, growing more discouraged with each passing sand dune. The Amalekites have a large lead and have left no clues. But then David hits the jackpot. "They found an Egyptian in the field, and brought him to David; and they gave him bread and he ate, and they let him drink water" (1 Samuel 30:11).

The Egyptian is a disabled servant who weighs more than he is worth, so the Amalekites had left him to starve in the desert. David's men nurse him back to life with figs and raisins and ask the servant to lead them to the campsite of his old cronies. He is happy to oblige.

David and his men swoop down upon the enemy like hawks on rats. Every Israelite woman and child is rescued. Every Amalekite either bites the dust or hits the trail, leaving precious plunder behind. David goes from scapegoat to hero, and the whooping and hollering begin.

The punch line, however, is yet to be read. To feel the full force of it, imagine the thoughts of some of the players in this story.

The rescued wives. You've just been snatched from your home and dragged through the desert. You've feared for your life and

clutched your kids. Then, one great day, the good guys raid the camp. Strong arms sweep you up and set you in front of a camel hump. You thank God for the SWAT team who snatched you and begin searching the soldiers' faces for your husband.

"Honey!" you yell. "Honey! Where are you?"

Your rescuer reins the camel to a halt. "Uh," he begins, "uh . . . your honey stayed at the camp."

"He did *what?*"

"He hung with the guys at Brook Besor."

I don't know if Hebrew women had rolling pins, but if they did, they might begin slapping them about this moment. "Besor, eh? I'll tell you who'll be sore."

The rescue squad. When David called, you risked your life. Now, victory in hand, you gallop back to Brook Besor. You crest the ridge overlooking the camp and see the two hundred men below.

"You leeches."

While you fought, they slept. You went to battle; they went to matinees and massage therapists. They shot eighteen holes and stayed up late playing poker.

You might feel the way some of David's men felt: "Because they did not go with us, we will not give them any of the spoil that we have recovered, except for every man's wife and children" (30:22).

Rescued wives: angry.

Rescuers: resentful.

And what about the two hundred men who had rested? Worms have higher self-esteem. They felt as manly as a lace doily.

A Molotov cocktail of emotions is stirred, lit, and handed to David. Here's how he defused it:

"Don't do that after what the LORD has given us. He has protected us and given us the enemy who attacked us. Who will listen to what you say? The share will be the same for the one who stayed with the supplies as for the one who went into battle. All will share alike."
—30:23–24 NCV

Note David's words that they "stayed with the supplies," as if this had been their job. They hadn't asked to guard supplies; they had wanted to rest. But David dignifies their decision to stay.

David did many mighty deeds in his life. He did many foolish deeds in his life. But perhaps the noblest was this rarely discussed deed: he honored the tired soldiers at Brook Besor.

◉ ◉ ◉

Some of it was wise. Some of it not so. But Sarah's self-declared time-out was certainly interesting—especially that way-too-short, what-was-I-thinking, pink hair experiment!

Time for herself was a luxury Sarah had never allowed herself before. And it was fun. Restful, too. Until, that is, restful somehow became . . . restless. *Hey, I'm supposed to be enjoying this. What happened?*

"When will you be through resting, Sarah?" her littlest sister had asked wistfully that morning.

When, indeed? Sarah wondered that night in the quiet of her room. How long *would* she sit on the sidelines of life?

Plink. Plink. Plink! Plink! Plink!

One by one, she gathered up the five smooth

stones that Phoebe's paw had flicked from their shelf to the floor. The gleaming bits of polished amethyst from a long-ago vacation Bible school class were one of her cat's favorite toys.

PROBLEM

Sarah scooped up the little Siamese and hugged her. "You know, Ms. Phoebe, if I didn't know better, I'd think you were giving me a hint. In case you're wondering, I already know what David would do about this *goliath* I've made for myself.

"He'd trust it to God—and so can I."

With a sigh of relief, Sarah put her problem in God's hands.

....

Sarah answered the ringing phone. On the other end of the line was her youth minister, whose service project was coming apart at the seams. He needed help.

"I know you're out of the game for a while, Sarah, but is there any chance you could find the time to—"

"Is tomorrow too soon?"

THE CONGREGATION AT BROOK BESOR

RESUMING THE CHASE

Someday somebody will read what David did and name their church The Congregation at Brook Besor. Isn't that what the church is intended to be? A place for soldiers to recover their strength?

In his great book about David, *Leap Over a Wall*, Eugene

Peterson tells of a friend who signs her letters, "Yours at the Brook Besor."[9] I wonder how many could do the same. Too tired to fight. Too ashamed to complain. While others claim victories, the weary sit in silence. How many sit at the Brook Besor?

If you are listed among them, here is what you need to know: It's okay to rest. Jesus is your David. He fights when you cannot. He goes where you cannot. He's not angry if you sit. Did he not invite, "Come off by yourselves; let's take a break and get a little rest" (Mark 6:31 MSG)?

Brook Besor blesses rest.

Brook Besor also cautions against arrogance. David knew the victory was a gift. Let's remember the same. Salvation comes like the Egyptian in the desert, a delightful surprise on the path. Unearned. Undeserved. Who are the strong to criticize the tired?

BREATH

BREATH

Are you weary? Catch your breath. We need your strength.

Are you strong? Reserve passing judgment on the tired. Odds are you'll

BREATH

need to plop down yourself. And when you do, Brook Besor is a good story to know.

BREATH

BREATH

BREATH

UNSPEAKABLE GRIEF

CHAPTER 8

You might hear the news from a policeman, "I'm sorry, he didn't survive the accident."

You might return a friend's call, only to be told, "The surgeon brought bad news."

Too many spouses have heard these words from grim-faced soldiers: "We regret to inform you . . ."

In such moments spring becomes winter, blue turns to gray, birds go silent, and the chill of sorrow settles in. It's cold in the valley of the shadow of death.

David's messenger isn't a policeman, friend, or soldier. He is a breathless Amalekite, with torn clothing and hair full of dirt, who stumbles into Camp Ziklag with the news: "The people have fled from the battle, many of the people are fallen and dead, and Saul and Jonathan his son are dead also" (2 Samuel 1:4).

Facing Your Giants

David knows the Hebrews are fighting the Philistines. He knows Saul and Jonathan are in for the battle of their lives. He's been awaiting the outcome. When the messenger presents David  with Saul's crown and bracelet, David has undeniable proof—Saul and Jonathan are dead.

Jonathan. Closer than a brother. He had saved David's life and sworn to protect his children.

Saul. God's chosen. God's anointed. Yes, he had hounded David. He had badgered David. But he was still God's anointed.

God's chosen king—dead.

David's best friend—dead.

Leaving David to face yet another giant, the giant of grief.

◉ ◉ ◉

"No-o-o-o!" It couldn't be true. How could they lie to her like that? The doctors, her parents, everybody! It had to be some kind of sick joke. No way could Lyssa be gone! No way . . .

But she was. There's just no way of arguing with the finality of the twisted metal and broken bodies that are left when church bus meets train. Jenna Gordon was stuck at home with the flu. Jenna's last words to her twin had been, "See you later." But now she never would.

Unspeakable Grief

Lyssa was dead. It might as well have been Jenna as well. How could she possibly survive with half of *herself* gone?

Jenna and Lyssa . . . Lyssa and Jenna . . . the Gordon twins. Two sides of the same coin, two halves of the same *egg*, they were a perfectly matched pair: Same slender gymnast bodies. Same determined chins. Same easily tickled funny bones. Same honey-blonde hair and eyes the exact color of maple syrup. Same—

Of course, that was only what they *looked* like on the outside. On the inside, just to keep things interesting (which they generally did), Jenna and Lyssa were as different—and necessary, each to the other—as night and day. That didn't mean, though, that there was any of that aggressive/passive, leader/follower twin stuff for these two. They were all harmony and balance.

Sometimes it was Lyssa's carefree enthusiasm that led the way. Other times, it was levelheaded Jenna's inventive imagination that came up with the most *interesting* plots and plans. Lyssa scattered prayers like confetti as she went her merry way. Jenna was the one who'd remind her that God already knew what they needed without their tugging at his sleeve every three seconds.

Jenna and Lyssa. See one, you'd see the other—exactly the way they liked things. More than sisters, they were best friends, too—meeting whatever came together. But that was over. Lyssa was gone. Now there was just Jenna to figure out what to do with this crushing burden of sadness that weighed her down into the very depths of grief.

RESUMING THE CHASE

We've felt the heavy hand of grief on our shoulders. Not in Ziklag, but in emergency rooms, hospitals, car wrecks, and on battlefields. And we, like David, have two choices: flee or face the giant.

Many choose to flee grief. Captain Woodrow Call urged young Newt to do so. In the movie *Lonesome Dove*, Call and Newt are part of an 1880s Texas-to-Montana cattle drive. When a swarm of water moccasins ended the life of Newt's best friend, Call offered bereavement counsel, Western-style. At the burial, in the shade of elms and the presence of cowboys, he advised: "Walk away from it."

What else can we do? The grave stirs such unspeakable hurt and unanswerable questions, we're tempted to turn and walk. Change the subject, avoid the issue. Work hard. Stay busy. Stay distant. Head north to Montana and don't look back.

Yet we pay a high price when we do. Bereavement comes from the word *reave*. Look up reave in the dictionary, and you'll read: "To take away by force, plunder, rob." Death robs you. The grave plunders moments and memories: birthdays, vacations, lazy walks, shared talks. You are bereaved because you've been robbed.

Normal is no more and never will be again. Just when you think the beast of grief is gone, you hear a song she loved or smell the cologne he wore or pass a restaurant where the two of you used to eat. The giant keeps showing up.

100

And the giant of grief keeps stirring up. Stirring up . . .

Anxiety. "Am I next?"

Guilt over what you said or didn't say.

Wistfulness. You see intact families and long for your brother . . . your sister . . . your mother . . . your father.

The giant stirs up insomnia, loss of appetite, forgetfulness, thoughts of suicide. Grief is not a mental illness, but it sure feels like one sometimes.

Captain Call didn't understand this.

Your friends don't understand this.

You may not understand this. But please try. Understand the gravity of your loss. You didn't lose at Monopoly or misplace your keys. You can't walk away from this. At some point, within minutes or months, you need to do what David did. Face your grief.

Upon hearing of the deaths of Saul and Jonathan, "David lamented" (2 Samuel 1:17). The warrior wept. The commander buried a bearded face in calloused hands and cried. He "ripped his clothes to ribbons. All the men with him did the same. They wept and fasted the rest of the day, grieving the death of Saul and his son Jonathan, and also the army of GOD and the nation Israel, victims in a failed battle" (1:11–12 MSG).

Wailing warriors covered the hills—a herd of men walking, moaning, weeping, and mourning. They tore clothing, pounded the ground, and exhaled hurt.

You need to do the same. Flush the hurt out of your heart and when the hurt returns, flush it again. Go ahead, cry a Mississippi.

Jesus did. Next to the tomb of his dear friend, "Jesus wept" (John 11:35). Why would he do such a thing? Does he not know of

Lazarus's impending resurrection? He's one declaration from seeing his friend exit the grave. He'll see Lazarus before dinner. Why the tears?

Amid the answers we think we know and the many we don't is this one: death stinks.

Death amputates a limb of your life. So Jesus wept. And in his tears we find permission to shed our own.

I won't cry. I won't! Jenna promised herself the day of the funeral. She was determined to get through her final farewell to her lost twin without making a spectacle of herself. Lyssa deserved better. Laughing, fun-loving Lyssa deserved better.

Jenna made sure she got it, sitting very still, very small, very quiet throughout the beautiful service she'd helped plan. There had been some small comfort in making sure that every last detail—the flowers, the music, the readings—was exactly what Lyssa would have chosen. (Though wouldn't her lighthearted twin have cracked up at the thought of planning her own funeral!)

At the very last minute, Jenna added one thing for herself: Isaiah's beautiful words about those who hope in the Lord soaring "on wings like eagles."[10] That was how she wanted to think of Lyssa—not the broken body pulled from the wreckage of the train-bus collision.

Unspeakable Grief

Jenna made it through the funeral. But after . . . ?

Life went on. But for the longest time, Jenna didn't. She was too empty . . . lost . . . *frozen* . . . to care much about anything.

Get back to normal? How could she? There would be no sophomore year for Lyssa. How could Jenna possibly enjoy her own?

Pick up the pieces of her life and move on? To what?

Crying would have helped, but she couldn't seem to do that, either. *Not even one tear? Not even THAT?!* she howled silently to herself. And that's when it happened: The ice cracked. The dam broke. The earth shook. And Jenna got MAD! Mad at life that promised so much and delivered so little. Mad at a world where such things could happen. Mad at . . . everything.

Sometimes she was even angry with Lyssa for leaving her. And she was absolutely *furious* with God! She didn't mind telling him so, either. Where was he when the train hit the church bus?! (*CHURCH bus, God. Remember? Your people!*) After the nonstop commentary Lyssa sent his way, how could he have forgotten about her? (*Weren't you LISTENING, God?*)

That last angry question stopped Jenna in her tracks. Of course God listened! She was the one who'd stopped listening for *him*. God hadn't forgotten Lyssa or abandoned *her*. Nor had he abandoned or forgotten Jenna. He was always there with whatever Jenna needed—long before Jenna knew she needed it. He'd see Jenna through this, too.

And that's when the tears came. Sometimes, in the weeks that followed, it seemed to Jenna that she would cry forever, but if that's what it took, that's what it took. A sister like Lyssa deserved no less.

JESUS WEPT

We don't know how long Jesus wept. We don't know how long David wept. But we know how long we weep, and the time seems so truncated. Egyptians dress in black for six months. Some Muslims wear mourning clothes for a year. Orthodox Jews offer prayers for a deceased parent every day for eleven months. Just fifty years ago, rural Americans wore black armbands for a period of several weeks.[11] And today? Am I the only one who senses that we hurry our hurts?

Grief takes time. Give yourself some. "Sages invest themselves in hurt and grieving" (Ecclesiastes 7:4 MSG). *Lament* may be a foreign verb in our world, but not in Scripture's. Seventy percent of the psalms are poems of sorrow. Why, the Old Testament includes a book of Lamentations. The son of David wrote: "Sorrow is better than laughter, for sadness has a refining influence on us" (Ecclesiastes 7:3 NLT).

We spelunk life's deepest issues in the cave of sorrow. Why am I here? Where am I headed? Cemetery strolls stir hard yet vital questions. David indulged the full force of his remorse: "I am worn out from sobbing. Every night tears drench my bed; my pillow is wet from weeping" (Psalm 6:6 NLT).

And then later: "I am dying from grief; my years

are shortened by sadness. Misery has drained my strength; I am wasting away from within" (Psalm 31:10 NLT).

Are you angry with God? Tell him. Disgusted with God? Let him know. Weary of telling people you feel fine, when you don't? Tell the truth. David did. And in the honesty of his pain, expressed in so many ways, he found healing.

◉ ◉ ◉

The language of grief is written differently for each mourner. For Jenna, her sorrow spoke through tears for days, for weeks, for months.

But there were other times, too—times when a remembered escapade or random memory of something Lyssa had said or done would surprise her into laughter. Best of all were the times when Jenna rediscovered her ability to laugh at herself. *That* happened while she was opening her umpteenth box of tissues. Out of nowhere—and certainly out of her own mouth—popped: "Well, there's sure no 'stiff upper lip' here!"

That phrase was a Lyssa classic. Her twin had discovered it in a very old movie on late-night cable. It was a costume epic about stalwart British *chaps* facing difficulties with stern fortitude. Whenever disaster would loom—which was often—someone was bound to say: "Stiff upper lip, old chap . . . stiff upper lip! Can't let the side down, you know."

It had cracked Lyssa up and soon became a catch phrase for

the two of them. Whenever they found themselves in a tricky or iffy situation—and often through the metal-mouthed trauma of braces—there it would come, in Lyssa's best pseudo-British accent: "Stiff upper lip, old chap . . . can't let the side down!"

But I am letting the side down! Jenna suddenly realized. Lyssa deserved so much better a memorial than this constant . . . wallowing . . . in what was gone. Her joyful, high-hearted twin would expect her to move forward and make something special of what was ahead. *And get on with it!*

So Jenna stuck out a stubborn chin and went toe-to-toe with grief. She cried when she had to, laughed when she could, and leaned on God all the way.

Yes, her sister . . . her other half . . . her best friend . . . was gone. But Jenna was still here, and she'd honor Lyssa's memory in the best way of all—by doing some of the things that had been closest to her sister's generous heart. Jenna started by continuing Lyssa's tradition of helping out at the local homeless shelter Thanksgiving week—and brought along with her the helping hands of her entire family and her church's youth group.

Lyssa might be gone, but Jenna would see to it that the light of Lyssa's bright spirit would shine on! When Jenna *did* see her sister again—and she knew she would in God's own time—she wanted to hear that *other* movie phrase Lyssa had been so fond of: "Good show, old chap . . . good show!"

DAVID WEPT

David refused to ignore his grief or hide his sorrow. He hurt, and he let it show.

> The mighty warriors—fallen, fallen!
> Women of Israel, weep for Saul. . . .
> O my dear brother Jonathan,
>   I'm crushed by your death.
> Your friendship was a miracle-wonder,
>   love far exceeding anything I've known—
>   or ever hope to know.
> The mighty warriors—fallen, fallen.
> —2 Samuel 1:19, 24, 26–27 MSG

David wept as creatively as he worshiped and—underline this—"David sang this lament over Saul and his son Jonathan, and gave orders that everyone in Judah learn it by heart" (2 Samuel 1:17–18 MSG).

David called the nation to mourning. He rendered weeping a public policy. He refused to gloss over or soft-pedal death. He faced it, fought it, challenged it. But he didn't deny it. As his son Solomon explained, "There is . . . a time to mourn" (Ecclesiastes 3:1, 4 NIV).

Give yourself some. Face your grief with tears; time; and one more, face your grief with truth. Paul urged the Thessalonians to grieve, but he didn't want the Christians to "carry on over them like people who have nothing to lookforward to, as if the grave were the last word" (1 Thessalonians 4:13 MSG).

God has the last word on death, and, if you listen, he will tell you the truth about your loved ones. They've been dismissed from the hospital called Earth. You and I still roam the halls, smell the medicines, and eat green beans and Jell-O off of plastic trays. They, meanwhile, enjoy picnics, inhale springtime, and run through knee-high flowers. You miss them like crazy, but can you deny the truth? They have no pain, doubt, or struggle. They really are happier in heaven.

And won't you see them soon? Life blisters by at mach speed. "You have made my days a mere handbreadth; the span of my years is as nothing before you. Each man's life is but a breath" (Psalm 39:5 NIV).

When your parents drop you off at school, do you weep like you'll never see them again? When you leave your friends at the mall, do you bid a final forever farewell? No. When you say, *"I'll see you soon,"* you mean it. When you stand in the cemetery and stare down at the soft, freshly turned earth and promise, "I'll see you soon," you speak truth. Reunion is a splinter of an eternal moment away.

There is no need for you to "grieve like the rest of men, who have no hope" (1 Thessalonians 4:13 NIV).

So go ahead, face your grief. Give yourself time. Permit yourself tears. God understands. He knows the sorrow of a grave. He buried his Son. But he also knows the joy of resurrection. And by his power, you will, too.

BLIND INTERSECTIONS

CHAPTER 9

I can get lost anywhere. Seriously, anywhere. The simplest map confuses me; the clearest trail bewilders me. I couldn't track an elephant through four feet of snow. I can misread instructions to the bathroom down the hall. Indeed, once I did and embarrassed several women in a fast-food restaurant in Fort Worth.

My list of mishaps reads like comedy ideas for the Pink Panther movies:

- I once got lost in my hotel. I told the receptionist my key wasn't working, only to realize I'd been on the wrong floor trying to open the wrong door.
- Several years ago I was convinced my car had been stolen from the airport parking garage. It hadn't; I was in the wrong garage.
- I once boarded the wrong flight and awoke in the wrong city.

- While in Seattle, I left my hotel in plenty of time for my speaking engagement, but when I saw highway signs advertising the Canadian border, I knew I'd be late.

- I once went for a morning jog, returned to the hotel, and ate. I'd finished two portions of the free buffet before I remembered: My hotel had no breakfast bar. I was in the wrong place.

If geese had my sense of direction, they'd spend winters in Alaska. I can relate to Columbus, who, as they say, didn't know where he was going when he left, didn't know where he was when he got there, and didn't know where he had been when he got back.

Can you relate? Of course you can. We've all scratched our heads a time or two, if not at highway intersections, at least at the crossroads of life. The best of navigators have wondered: Do I

- try for college or give up?

- accept that questionable date or pass?

- listen to my parents or tune them out?

- take a stand or back off?

One of life's giant-sized questions is: *How can I know what God wants me to do?* And David asks it. After years of exile, he's just learned of the deaths of Saul and Jonathan. Suddenly the throne is empty and David's options are open. But before he steps out, he looks up:

> It happened after this that David inquired of the LORD, saying, "Shall I go up to any of the cities of Judah?" And the LORD said to him, "Go up." David said, "Where shall I go up?" And He said, "To Hebron." —2 Samuel 2:1

David makes a habit of running his options past God. And he does so with a fascinating tool. The ephod. Trace its appearance to David's initial escape from Saul. David seeks comfort from the priests of Nob. Saul accuses the priests of harboring the fugitive and, consistent with Saul's paranoia, he murders them all. One priest by the name of Abiathar, however, flees. He escapes with more than just his life; he escapes with the ephod.

> After Abiathar took refuge with David, he joined David in the raid on Keilah, bringing the Ephod with him. . . .
>
> David got wind of Saul's strategy to destroy him and said to Abiathar the priest, "Get the Ephod." Then David prayed to GOD: "God of Israel, I've just heard that Saul plans to come to Keilah and destroy the city because of me. Will the city fathers of Keilah turn me over to him? Will Saul come down and do what I've heard? O GOD, God of Israel, tell me!"
>
> GOD replied, "He's coming down."
>
> "And will the head men of Keilah turn me and my men over to Saul?" And GOD said, "They'll turn you over." So David and his men got out of there. —1 Samuel 23:6, 9–13 MSG

David dons the ephod, speaks to God, and receives an answer. Something similar occurs after the destruction of Ziklag. With his village in ruins and his men enraged,

He ordered Abiathar the priest, son of Ahimelech, "Bring me the Ephod so I can consult God." Abiathar brought it to David. Then David prayed to GOD, "Shall I go after these raiders? Can I catch them?" The answer came, "Go after them! Yes, you'll catch them! Yes, you'll make the rescue!" —30:7–8 MSG

What is happening? What is this ephod? What makes it so effective? And are they sold in department stores?

EPHODS
$20

◉ ◉ ◉

If ever someone was "born under the sign of the question mark" (as his mother laughingly insisted), it was Cody Blake. From the moment he'd first opened fascinated blue eyes on the world—and immediately set about figuring it all out—it was the question mark that summed up Cody's approach to life. His favorite question was "why?" followed by "how?" then on to "what?" and "what if?"—with Cody in immediate hot pursuit of the answers such queries demanded. Just ask his mom.

While other toddlers dropped food from their highchairs by accident, or sometimes for fun, it struck her that Cody was systematically exploring gravity. Of course, that *could* have been just a typical proud-mom assumption. The fifth time she had to pluck him from the top of the bookcase, where he was testing the theory from greater heights, she was sure. A later experiment with gravity—or was it man-powered flight?—which involved a bath-towel cape, the porch roof, and a trip to the emergency room at age four, was considerably more nerve-racking. As were his early examinations of things electrical and mechanical. But his parents had long since kid-proofed the house, prayed for an extra-alert guardian angel, and resigned themselves to a white-knuckle childhood.

Cody-the-Curious hadn't changed a bit in the years between childhood and high school. He had yet to meet a mystery he didn't like. Endlessly inquisitive, Cody simply couldn't resist the slightest whiff of any puzzle, enigma, conundrum, or uncharted territory. Whatever it was—around the next corner, behind the next door, inside the next experience—he simply had to *KNOW*!

By ninth grade, he had already acquired an impressive fund of miscellaneous information about all kinds of fascinating things. But there's one thing he never had caught on to: There are times when following your curiosity—with no reliable guide to the wisdom of what you're doing—can leave you wandering in some very strange territory.

MYSTERY

The mysterious ephod that David relied on for guidance originated in the era of wilderness wanderings. Moses presented the first one to Aaron, the priest. It was an ornate vest, woven of white linen, embroidered with threads of blue, purple, scarlet, and gold. A breast-plate bearing twelve precious stones adorned the vest. The breastplate contained one or two, maybe three, resplendent diamonds or diamondlike stones. These stones had the names Urim and Thummim. No one knows the exact meaning of the terms, but "light" and "perfection" lead the list.

God revealed his will to the priests through these stones. How? Ancient writers have suggested several methods. The stones:

- illuminated when God said yes;
- contained moving letters that gathered to form a response;
- were sacred lots that, upon being cast, would reveal an answer.[12]

While we speculate on the technique, we don't need to guess at the value. Would you not cherish such a tool? When faced with a puzzling choice, David could, with reverent heart, make a request and God would answer.

Will Saul come after me? He will.
Will the men capture me? They will.
Should I pursue the enemy? You should.
Will I overtake them? You will.

Oh, that God would do the same for us. That we could ask and he would answer. That we could cry out and he would reply.

Wouldn't you love to have an ephod? Who's to say you don't? God hasn't changed. He still promises to guide us:

> The LORD says, "I will guide you along the best pathway for your life. I will advise you and watch over you." —Psalm 32:8 NLT
>
> Seek his will in all you do, and he will direct your paths. —Proverbs 3:6 NLT
>
> Whether you turn to the right or to the left, your ears will hear a voice behind you, saying, "This is the way; walk in it." —Isaiah 30:21 NIV

The God who guided David guides you. You simply need to consult your Maker. I wish I'd sought counsel before I made a recent decision. When searching for some breakfast early one morning, I spotted a Baggie of cookies in the kitchen. Denalyn and Sara had just attended a school bake sale, so I thought, *What great luck! Breakfast cookies. Denalyn must have set them out for me.*

I ate one and found it very chewy, almost gummy. *Interesting texture*, I thought. *Reminds me of pita bread.* I ate a second. The taste was a bit subtle for my preference, but when mixed with coffee, it made for an interesting option. I grabbed a third for the road. I would have grabbed the fourth, but only one remained, so I left it for Denalyn.

Later in the day, she phoned. "Looks like someone has been in the bag."

"It was me," I admitted. "I've had better breakfast cookies, but those weren't bad."

"Those weren't breakfast cookies, Max."

"They weren't?"

"No."

"What were they?"

"Homemade dog biscuits."

"Oh . . ." That explained a lot. That explained the gummy texture and the tasteless taste. That also explained why all day each time I scratched my belly my leg kicked (not to mention my sudden interest in fire hydrants).

I should've consulted the maker. We need to consult ours. And it's easier to do than you may think.

◉ ◉ ◉

Even for someone like Cody Blake—who was expert at navigating the unknown—the move up to high school comes complete with possibilities (to make a major splash) *and* pitfalls (to trip the unwary).

Cody, of course, jumped right in—never stopping to consider that the shifting sands of ninth grade might be as treacherous as they were tantalizing. The issue of whether he'd impress or flop was a minor detail. The important thing was to know more *after* than he did *before*.

YADA
YADA
YADA

Without realizing it, Cody arrived on the scene well-prepared to impress. His eclectic interests, sharp research skills, and bone-deep determination to find the answer to *anything* practically guaranteed academic success—not to mention entertaining, if offbeat, lunchtime conversations. Cody could talk to just about anyone about just about anything. And did.

Push the right button and get a crash course on: Codes and code-breaking. The science of invisibility. The possibility of "wormholes" in space as shortcuts from galaxy to galaxy. The reason for the shifting golden fires inside tiger's-eye quartz (using his own to demonstrate). The secrets of building everything from the Great Pyramid to sky-scrapers designed to sway with the wind. How to assemble a model ship inside a bottle. The real scoop on the Indian Rope Trick, Houdini's escapes, and other illusionist mysteries. And that was just for starters.

It was also *before* . . . before, out of the blue, came the most intriguing mystery of all: girls. As *EUREKA!* moments go, it ranked right up there with the world-shaking effects of a polar shift. (Cody could tell you all about *those*, too.) Oh, it wasn't big news to him that there was another gender. He'd had a lot of friends over the years who just happened to be girls. But his focus had always been on the contents rather than the packaging. All it took to shake up that point of view was one teasing sidelong glance from Emily Martin's golden-brown eyes.

Almost overnight the pursuit of knowledge gave way to a sud-denly more important issue: How to impress girls! Especially one girl. Cody threw himself into that challenge with (what he thought was) a stroke-of-genius strategy: Hang out with guys girls were impressed by! But *which* guys? The cool confidence of leadership wasn't his strong suit. Nor were the flamboyant antics of the class clown. He had zero athletic skills, so that left out jock-dom. He definitely *could* fit in with "the smart kids," but what he had in mind was something more . . . distinctive. Which left the more mysterious types, whose aura of amused sophistication hinted at unspecified delights . . . and dangers. A risky direction to choose? Maybe. But how would he ever know for sure, unless he checked it out for himself?

Discover your Maker's direction for your life by marinating your mind in his writing.

Maybe you have no Urim and Thummim stones, but:

You have a Bible? Read it.

Has any other book ever been described in this fashion? "For the word of God is living and active. Sharper than any double-edged sword, it penetrates even to dividing soul and spirit, joints and marrow; it judges the thoughts and attitudes of the heart" (Hebrews 4:12 NIV).

"Living and active." The words of the Bible have life! Nouns with pulse rates. Muscular adjectives. Verbs darting back and forth across the page. God works through these words. The Bible is to God what a surgical glove is to the surgeon. He reaches through them to touch deep within you.

Haven't you felt his touch?

In a late, lonely hour, you read the words: "I will never fail you. I will never forsake you" (Hebrews 13:5 NLT). The sentences comfort like a hand on your shoulder.

When worry eats away at your peace, someone shares this passage: "Do not be anxious about anything, but in everything, by prayer and petition, with thanksgiving, present your requests to God" (Philippians 4:6 NIV). The words stir a sigh from your soul.

Or perhaps laziness is knocking on your door. You're considering a halfhearted effort when Colossians 3:23 comes to mind: "Whatever you do, work at it with all your heart, as working for the Lord, not for men" (NIV). Such words can cut, can't they?

Put them to use. "Let the words of Christ, in all their richness, live in your hearts and make you wise. Use his words to teach and counsel each other" (Colossians 3:16 NLT).

Don't make a decision, whether large or small, without sitting before God with open Bible, open heart, open ears, imitating the prayer of Samuel: "Your servant is listening" (1 Samuel 3:10 NLT).

You have a family of faith? Consult it.

Others have asked your question. You aren't the first to face your problem. Someone else has stood where you stand and wondered what you wonder. Seek their advice.

You don't need an ephod to wear or stones to consult; you have God's family. He will speak to you through it. And, he will speak to you through your own conscience.

You have a heart for God? Heed it.

Christ nudges the Christ-possessed heart. "God is working in you to help you want to do and be able to do what pleases him" (Philippians 2:13 NCV). What does your heart tell you to do? What choice creates the greatest sense of peace?

Sometimes a choice just "feels" right. When Luke—who had never actually met Jesus—justified the writing of his Gospel to Theophilus, he said: "Since I myself have carefully investigated everything from the beginning, it seemed good also to me to write an orderly account for you, most excellent Theophilus" (Luke 1:3 NIV).

Did you note the phrase "it seemed good also to me"? These words reflect a person standing at the crossroads. Luke pondered his options and selected the path that "seemed good."

Jude did likewise. He intended to make his epistle about the topic of salvation, but he felt uneasy with the choice. Look at the third verse of his letter:

> "Dear friends, I wanted very much to write you about the salvation we all share. But I felt the need to write you about something else: I want to encourage you to fight hard for the faith that was given the holy people of God once and for all time." —Jude 1:3 NCV

Again, the language. "I wanted very much to . . . But I felt . . ." From whence came Jude's feelings? Did they not come from God? The same God who "is working in you to help you want to do . . . what pleases him" (Philippians 2:13 NCV).

God creates the "want to" within us.

Be careful with this. People have been known to justify stupidity based on a feeling. "I felt God leading me to cheat on that test . . . break my promise . . . lie to my parents . . . go to that rave." Mark it down: God will not lead you to violate his Word. He will not contradict his teaching. Be careful with  the phrase "God led me . . ." Don't banter it about. Don't disguise your sin as a leading of God. He will not lead you to lie, cheat, or hurt. He will faithfully lead you through the words of his Scripture and the advice of his faithful.

◉ ◉ ◉

It *seemed* like a good idea at the time: Cody's master plan to impress Emily Martin with an intriguing change of image as a *sophisticated* risktaker. If that meant trying on a mind-set and lifestyle completely outside of his experience, what could it hurt?

Cody might have known a lot about a lot of things, but he still had a lot more to learn. Smart as he was at tracking down the most obscure information, it had never occurred to him to use those same analytical skills to look at the *real* world. It had also never crossed his mind that not everyone—and not every experiment— is necessarily harmless, and not every out-come is the one you expect.

Actually, Emily might have liked the *real* Cody just fine, if she'd been given the chance to find out. But he was so preoccupied try-ing to fit in with his new crowd that the opportunity never came up.

Not that his personality transplant was going all that well. He *did* come close to the required attitude of amused indifference to consequences. But it didn't fit him any better than the slick new wardrobe that never felt quite right, either. And when Emily did seem to notice him, he was never sure if the look in her eyes was interest . . . or disappointment.

Cody was feeling quite a lot of disappointment himself—and even more uneasiness. His new friends weren't quite as "with it" as he'd thought at first. Their dashing quest for new experiences turned out to be less about knowledge than sensation. He'd managed to convince himself—for a while—that taking a quick peek at the forbidden "just to see what all the fuss was about" couldn't be all that bad. But as one thing led to another . . . and another . . . it didn't take Cody long to realize that his curiosity was dangerously close to morphing into stupidity. Naive he might be, but he certainly wasn't that dumb!

So, no longer the old Cody, and not liking the new Cody at all— he did the only thing he could do. He bowed out as gracefully as possible, which left him nowhere in particular—stuck at the intersection of What Was I Thinking? and Where Do I Go From Here?

Too bad life doesn't come with an instruction book. (*Or does it?*) Mixed in with some change he was taking out of his pocket was the tiger's-eye stone, which reminded him of the four other stones at home and David's story. And Cody realized he had completely forgotten about the most important question of all: What kind of *person* did he want to be?

Well, he knew exactly where to find the answer. It *would* be embarrassing, of course, to show up—out of the blue—after far

122

too long an absence. But there was one place that always had room at the table for a prodigal returned: church.

That Sunday Cody felt more than just welcomed; he felt . . . at home. Questions and all, he was exactly where he should be. And glad to be there.

And that was *before* the close of service brought him a beautiful surprise: a smiling glance and a warm hello from Emily Martin.

DIRECTION FOR YOUR LIFE

You need no ephod or precious stones to help you find your way; you have a heart in which God's Spirit dwells. As F. B. Meyer wrote a century ago:*

> Each child of God has his own Urim and Thummim stones, . . . a conscience void of offense, a heart cleansed in the blood of Christ, a spiritual nature which is pervaded and filled by the Holy Spirit of God. . . . Are you in difficulty about your way? Go to God with your question; get direction from the light of his smile or the cloud of his refusal. . . . Get alone, where the lights and shadows of earth cannot interfere, where the disturbance of self-will does not intrude, where human opinions fail to reach . . . wait there silent and expectant, though all around you insist on immediate decision or action—the will of God will be made clear; and you will have . . . a new conception of God, [and] a deeper insight into his nature.[13]

You have a heart for God? Heed it.

A family of faith? Consult it.

A Bible? Read it.

You have all you need to face the giant-sized questions of your life. Most of all, you have a God who loves you too much to let you wander. Trust him . . . and avoid the dog biscuits.

CHAPTER 10

Pete sits in the empty gym and leans his head against the wall. He'd like to bang his head against it. He just messed up again. Everyone misspeaks occasionally. Pete and his foot-in-mouth do so daily. If he thinks it, he says it—blurting sarcastic comments like a whale spouts salt water, without thought for the fallout. His clever, caustic comments always hurt someone, but today he hurt his best friend. Oh, Pete and his quick-triggered tongue.

Then there's Jon and his disastrous classroom performance. Smart enough to succeed, sloppy enough to fail, the poor guy just can't get his act together. His academic career rivals the Rocky Mountains—up, down; cold, hot; lush, barren. His early knack for math fell victim to his erratic study habits. Procrastination shelved his gift for storytelling—and English grade—"until I have time." History class seemed promising, until

UP

DOWN

"all those names and dates to remember" got in the way. And so on through the rest of the curriculum: Promising starts. Disappointing finishes. Now he's on academic probation, future as bleak as the Mojave Desert. No one could fault him for feeling insecure, he's flopped at each opportunity.

So has Carol, not at grades, but at friendships. She's been trying since kinder- garten to make, and keep, friends. But she just can't seem to figure out how to go about it. Sometimes she tries so hard she makes people uncomfortable. Other times, she misses promising opportunities by not trying at all. Then when she does make a rare connection, she usually manages to sabotage it in some way. She comes across as too needy, too independent, too pushy, too aloof, too agreeable, too indifferent . . . Carol seems destined for a life of relationship flops.

People and their proverbial hang-ups. Pete always speaks before he thinks. Jon always fails where he should succeed. Carol wins at friendship as often as a burro wins at the Kentucky Derby.

And you. Does one prevailing problem leech your life?

Some are prone to cheat. Others quick to doubt. Maybe you worry. Yes, everyone worries some, but you own the national distrib- utorship of anxiety. Perhaps you are judgmental. Sure, everybody can be critical, but you pass more judgments than a federal judge.

What is that one weakness, bad habit, rotten attitude? Where does Satan have a stronghold on you? Ahh, there is the fitting word—*stronghold*: a fortress, a citadel, thick walls, tall gates. It's as if the devil staked a claim on one weakness and constructed a rampart around it. "You ain't touching this flaw," he defies to heaven, placing himself squarely between God's help and your

- explosive temper,
- fragile self-image,
- freezer-sized appetite,
- distrust for authority.

Seasons come and go, and this Loch Ness monster still lurks in the water-bottom of your soul. He won't go away. He lives up to both sides of his compound name: *strong* enough to grip like a vise and stubborn enough to *hold* on. He clamps like a bear trap—the harder you shake, the more it hurts.

Strongholds: old, difficult, discouraging challenges. We all face them.

◉ ◉ ◉

It was fortunate that Cassie Hamilton liked challenges. Who'd have dreamed her new leg—an engineering marvel of space-age materials and human ingenuity—would turn out to be as stubborn, and set on going its own way, as Cassie herself? But there it was, part promise and part dare. And there was Cassie, chin tilted, gray eyes determined.

Thanks to her quirky friend Mia, she'd made it through those first awful weeks after her personal disaster—and she wasn't going to give up now!

Facing Your Giants

For Cassie, there had always been only one way to go and that was full speed ahead. A star athlete all through middle and early high school, she had all the gifts: Blazing speed. Flawless technique. A champion's grit and determination. Even as a rising sophomore, college scouts were taking notice. Then—  catastrophe!—a carelessly driven speedboat transformed Cassie-the-*Someday*-Olympian into Cassie-the-*Might-Have-Been*.

Now here she was at another starting line—with only one good leg to take her where she needed to go. But she'd get there. No matter what it took!

With a flip of her trademark braid of copper-colored hair, Cassie gripped the parallel walking rails for the umpteenth time and leaned forward. "Okay, let's try this again!"

"You go, girl!" called Mia from her director's chair on the sidelines. "*This* time—if I may venture a suggestion—*forward*, instead of down."

Cassie grinned and shifted her weight onto her contrary prosthesis. "Picky. Picky. Picky. Everybody's a critic."

Then, with the confidence of someone who felt a strong and loving arm around her shoulders—as she had ever since that turning-point night when she'd reconnected with her God—Cassie took a step. Then another. And another. *Piece of cake!* And one mor—*Ooops!*

"Sorry, Jim," said Cassie, pulling herself upright. "I think the alignment is out again. Or I am."

"Not a problem," came the cheerful answer from the technician responsible for fitting and endlessly adjusting Cassie's complicated new leg. "It might take a while," he said, digging through his tool kit, "but I'll get it. And so will you."

"You know I will! If you've got the way, Jim, I've got the *will*," quipped Cassie.

ULTIMATE CHALLENGE

When it came to strongholds, David faced the ultimate challenge when he looked at Jerusalem. When you and I think of the city, we envision temples and prophets. We picture Jesus teaching and a New Testament church growing. We imagine a thriving, hub-of-history capital.

When David sees Jerusalem in 1000 BC, he sees something else. He sees a millennium-old cheerless fortress, squatting defiantly on the spine of a ridge of hills. A rugged outcropping elevates her. Tall walls protect her. Jebusites indwell her. No one bothers them. Philistines fight the Amalekites. Amalekites fight the Hebrews. But the Jebusites? They are a coiled rattlesnake in the desert. Everyone leaves them alone.

Everyone, that is, except David. The just-crowned king of Israel has his eye on Jerusalem. He's inherited a divided kingdom. The people need not just a strong leader, but strong headquarters. David's present base of Hebron sits too far south to enlist the loyalties of the northern tribes. But if he moves north, he'll isolate the south. He seeks a neutral, centralized city.

He wants Jerusalem. We can only wonder how many times he's stared at her walls. He grew up in Bethlehem, only a day's walk to the south. He hid in the caves in the region of En Gedi, not far south. Surely he noticed Jerusalem. Somewhere he pegged the place as the perfect capital. The crown had scarcely been resized for his head when he set his eyes on his newest goliath.

> And the king and his men went to Jerusalem against the Jebusites, the inhabitants of the land, who spoke to David, saying, "You shall not come in here; but the blind and the lame will repel you." . . . Nevertheless David took the stronghold of Zion (that is, the City of David). Now David said on that day, "Whoever climbs up by way of the water shaft and defeats the Jebusites . . . he shall be chief and captain." . . . Then David dwelt in the stronghold, and called it the City of David. —2 Samuel 5:6–9

This regrettably brief story teases us with the twofold appearance of the term *stronghold*. In verse 7, "David took the stronghold," and in verse 9, "David dwelt in the stronghold."

Jerusalem meets the qualifications of one: an old, difficult, and discouraging fortress. From atop the turrets, Jebusite soldiers have ample time to direct arrows at any would-be wall climbers. And discouraging? Just listen to the way the city dwellers taunt David: "You'll never get in here. . . . Even the blind and lame could keep you out!" (5:6 NLT).

The Jebusites pour scorn on David like Satan dumps buckets of discouragement on you.

- "You'll never overcome your bad habits."
- "Born a loser, gonna die a loser."
- "Think you can conquer your hang-ups? Think again."

If you've heard the mocking that David heard, your story needs the word that David's has. Did you see it? Most hurry past it. Let's not. Pull out a pen and underline this twelve-letter masterpiece.

Nevertheless.

"Nevertheless David took the stronghold. . . ."

Granted, the city was old. The walls were difficult. The voices were discouraging . . . *nevertheless* David took the stronghold. But it's how he did it that's the real story.

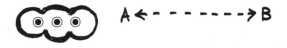

"I've got a new one for us, Cass," announced Mia as she entered Cassie's room. Mia was "into" mottos (though not yet the pizza box she'd been struggling to open). "*Nevertheless!* How's *that* for a word with a stubborn chin and a glint in its eye?"

"Nevertheless?" echoed Cassie, just doubtfully enough to push Mia's buttons.

"Absolutely," insisted Mia. "It's the 'never mind all that' approach to the bumps in the road between point A and point B. What could be better for *us*?"

Then Cassie's smile, back from temporary vacation, broke free. "Perfect," she agreed. "So is your timing." *Or God's?*

After this not-so-successful day, what could be better than sharing a pizza with Mia for dinner? "Actually, I've been expecting you."

Cassie wasn't sure exactly how it worked, but whenever her demon of discouragement stopped in to set up shop, hard on his heels would be Mia.

Mia, the unquenchable, who was fighting a gallant battle of her own with the crippling effects of juvenile arthritis. Mia, the pint-sized philosopher, whose gifts to Cassie were laughter and inspiration.

"Really, Cass," she'd said once, "why should I fret just because I can no longer . . . *fret*?" Then, with an airy gesture of the gnarled fingers that had once drawn such amazing music from her violin, "If I focus too much on what's gone, I might miss seeing the next good thing God sends my way."

And so it had gone since their first meeting: An *up* for every *down*. Lots of pizza. And always when Cassie most needed it, a feeling that she was on her way to some special *something*. That kept her courage high as she dug into challenge after challenge: Coming to terms with her loss. The impatient wait for her stump (*Stump?! Yuck!*) to heal. Fighting to regain balance and coordination in a body missing part of itself. *And now, just to make things really interesting, this awkward dance with a not-so-cooperative new leg that insists on leading!*

With that last thought, Cassie started laughing. "Wouldn't you know, *I'd* get the diva-of-a-leg!"

"Well," said Mia helpfully, "maybe she just wants to show her stuff, so you can show yours. Why not make friends?"

She?! A leg with both gender and agenda? There it was again: that quirky Mia point of view that shifted perspectives—and moved mountains. *Make friends?!*

As they demolished the pizza, Cassie's busy brain turned the idea inside out and upside down. The more she looked at it, the more promising it seemed. Her sophisticated new leg was a marvel of possibilities. Why not make friends with it? Why not transform this newest challenge into one more shining *nevertheless* in the story she and God were writing together?

"Yes! Why *not?!*"

Mia jumped as Cassie's decisive words broke the long silence. "Why not' what?" she asked.

Cassie shrugged. "Oh, just a thought," she said, tapping her prosthesis. "Why not take Liz here for a walk? You know, a little road work."

"Liz?" echoed a puzzled Mia.

"Sure," came the answer. "Liz, as in—get ready, here it comes— nevertheless LIZ!"

NEVERTHELESS

Wouldn't you love God to write a *nevertheless* in your biography? Born to alcoholics, *nevertheless* she led a sober life. Never went to college, *nevertheless* he mastered a trade. Didn't read the Bible until retirement age, *nevertheless* he came to a deep and abiding faith.

We all need a *nevertheless*. And God has plenty to go around. Strongholds mean nothing to him. Remember Paul's words? "We use God's mighty weapons, not mere worldly weapons, to knock down the Devil's strongholds" (2 Corinthians 10:4 NLT).

You and I fight with toothpicks; God comes with battering rams and cannons. What he did for David, he can do for us. The question is, will we do what David did? The king models much here.

David turns a deaf ear to old voices. Those mockers strutting on the wall tops? David ignores them. He dismisses their words and goes on about his work.

Nehemiah, on these same walls, took an identical approach. In his case, however, he was atop the stones, and the mockers stood at the base. Fast-forward five hundred years, and you will see that the bulwarks of Jerusalem are in ruins, and many of her people are in captivity. Nehemiah heads a building program to restore the fortifications. Critics tell him to stop. They plan to interfere with his work. They list all the reasons the stones can't and shouldn't be restacked. But Nehemiah won't

listen to them. "I am doing a great work, so that I cannot come down. Why should the work cease while I leave it and go down to you?" (Nehemiah 6:3). Nehemiah knew how to press the mute button on his critics.

Jesus did, too. He responded to Satan's temptation with three terse sentences and three Bible verses. He didn't dialogue with the devil. When Peter told Christ to sidestep the cross, Jesus wouldn't entertain the thought. "Get behind Me, Satan!" (Matthew 16:23). A crowd of people ridiculed what he said about a young girl: "'The girl is not dead, only asleep.' But the people laughed at him" (9:24 NCV). You know what Jesus did with the naysayers? He silenced them. "After the crowd had been thrown out of the house, Jesus went into the girl's room and took hold of her hand, and she stood up" (9:25 NCV).

David, Nehemiah, and Jesus practiced selective listening. Can't we do the same?

Two types of thoughts continually vie for your attention. One says, "Yes, you can." The other says, "No, you can't." One

YOU CAN!   **YOU CAN'T!**

says, "God will help you." The other lies, "God has left you." One speaks the language of heaven; the other deceives in the slang of the Jebusites. One proclaims God's strengths; the other lists your failures. One longs to build you up; the other seeks to tear you down. And here's the great news: you select the voice you hear. Why listen to the mockers? Why heed their voices? Why give ear to pea-brains and scoffers when you can, with the same ear, listen to the voice of God?

CHOOSE ONE:
☐ GOD
☐ MOCKER

"Cassie . . ."

"Hi, Cassie . . ."

"Look, it's Cassie and Liz!"

Cassie and her leg-named-Liz became familiar sights in every nook and cranny of the medical center in the weeks and months following her pizza-fueled epiphany. She'd learned the place by heart as she'd traveled its endless corridors—first with slow, awkward steps, then smooth, confident strides, and now today's frisky trot.

She usually passed silently by with a quick grin and friendly wave, rarely interrupting her relentless roadwork to linger long anywhere. Anywhere, that is, but here, her favorite place of all. A megawatt smile lighting her face, Cassie took a sweeping bow and pranced into the pediatric cancer wing. "Boy, have I got a story for you guys today!"

Cassie absolutely couldn't resist those sweet, funny—brave—little kids who put up with so much for so long! What was losing just one leg compared to that? Many of them would never leave this place, but they'd be with Cassie *wherever* she went.

Facing Your Giants

They ran with Cassie—their bright spirits tucked in her heart—one glorious spring day nearly two years after her accident.

In the just-emptied locker room—she'd waited for that solitary time on purpose—Cassie changed clothes and laced on her running shoes. With a good-luck pat for her leg —*Okay, Liz, let's go for it!*—she was on her way to join her team. Oh, not the team she'd competed with for so many years (although some were there, too); this was her new team: a team whose only goal was to raise money for the pediatric cancer wing.

She wouldn't be the first, or fastest, to the finish line that day, but she was in the race! To the cheers of her teammates and family—and a whoop of delight from Mia in the stands—Cassie Hamilton was back on track.

....

"So, what's next, Cass?" Mia asked over lunch that weekend. "Tap-dancing?"

"Actually," said Cassie, "I was thinking more along the lines of triathlon. Someday. Might be kind of hard, though, to find time for biking, swimming, running, *and* tap-dancing.

"Unless, of course, I run into another . . ."

Cassie waited, then grinned as Mia chimed in, ". . . nevertheless!"

CLAIM YOUR NEVERTHELESS

To claim your nevertheless, do what David did. Turn a deaf ear to old voices. And, as you do, open your eyes to new choices. Where everyone else saw walls, David saw tunnels. Others focused on the obvious; David searched for the unusual. Since he did what no one expected, he achieved what no one imagined. Get creative with your problem solving.

One woman I know counters her anxiety by memorizing long sections of Scripture. A traveling sales rep asks the hotels to remove the television from his room so he won't be tempted to watch adult movies. Another man grew so weary of his prejudice that he moved into a minority neighborhood, made new friends, and changed his attitude.

If the wall is too tall, try a tunnel.

David found fresh hope in a hole outside the Jerusalem walls. So can you. Not far from David's tunnel lies the purported tomb of Christ. What David's tunnel did for him, the tomb of Jesus can do for you. "God's power is very great for us who believe. That power is the same as the great strength God used to raise Christ from the dead and put him at his right side in the heavenly world" (Ephesians 1:19–20 NCV).

Do what David did.

Turn a deaf ear to the old voices.

Open a wide eye to the new choices.

Who knows, you may be a prayer away from a *nevertheless*. God loves to give them.

TOUGH PROMISES

CHAPTER 11

King David's life couldn't be better. Just crowned. His throne room smells like fresh paint, and his city architect is laying out new neighborhoods. God's ark indwells the tabernacle; gold and silver overflow the king's coffers; Israel's enemies maintain their distance. The days of ducking Saul are a distant memory.

But something stirs one of them. A comment, perhaps, resurrects an old conversation. Maybe a familiar face jars a dated decision. In the midst of his new life, David remembers a promise from his old one: "Is there still anyone who is left of the house of Saul, that I may show him kindness for Jonathan's sake?" (2 Samuel 9:1).

Confusion furrows the faces of David's court. Why bother with the children of Saul? This is a new era, a new administration. Who cares about the old guard? David does. He does because he remembers the covenant he made with Jonathan. When Saul threatened to kill David, Jonathan sought to save him. Jonathan succeeded and then made this request: "If I make it through this alive, continue to be my covenant friend. And if I die, keep the covenant friendship with my family—forever" (1 Samuel 20:14–15 MSG).

Jonathan does die. But David's covenant does not. No one would have thought twice had he let it die. David has many reasons to forget the vow he made with Jonathan.

The two were young and idealistic. Who keeps the promises of youth?

Saul was cruel and relentless. Who honors the children of a nemesis?

David had a nation to rule and an army to lead. What king has time for small matters?

But to David, a covenant is no small matter. When you catalog the giants David faced, be sure the word *promise* survives the cut and makes the short list. It certainly appears on most lists of Everestish challenges.

Maybe you've tripped over—or been tripped up by—a few promises yourself. Sooner or later, we all have our encounters with promises.

Promises to stay true to . . . be there for . . . no matter what!

Promises to do—or not do—this or that, made in an excess of optimistic confidence.

Promises to others . . . to ourselves . . . to God.

Promises that sometimes, when push comes to shove, turn out to be easier said than done.

◉ ◉ ◉

It would be easy to be jealous of a guy like Brad Morelli—if he weren't so annoyingly likeable!

In fact, it's truly amazing that the green-eyed monster rarely shows up at all to rain on his parade. Brad not only seems to "have it all," he actually *does*: A friendly smile and easygoing manner that let him fit comfortably into just about any group or situation. Grades consistently on the high side of "good," even nudging "excellent" at times. Across-the-board athletic skills that make him a welcome addition to most any team he wants to join. And a positive *genius* for wearing, saying, and doing exactly the right thing at exactly the right time.

If Brad has one claim to fame that outranks all the others, it's his absolute reliability. Everyone knows you can count on Brad to do whatever it is he says he'll do. Every time. When he says, "No problem, I'll take care of it," whatever he's agreed to absolutely, positively will happen. Brad truly *is* as good as his word.

It's something he picked up from his dad. Tony Morelli—father, firefighter, hero—always believed that keeping your word, no matter how hard that might be to do, was "a matter of honor."

Honor was a word Brad heard often throughout his growing-up years. It was one of the rare things that his lighthearted, master-jokester of a dad took very seriously indeed. Honor covered a lot of territory in Brad's father's book of life, including obligations to family, friends, God . . . and yourself. Right at the top of *that* list was the matter of promises.

Tough Promises

Even today—years after his hero dad had run back into a burning building and traded his life for that of a trapped buddy—Brad could still hear him say it: "Easy or not, a promise is a promise. An honorable man keeps his word, son."

PROMISES PLEDGED

Promises. Pledged amid spring flowers. Cashed in February grayness. They loom Gulliver-sized over our Lilliputian lives. We never escape their shadow. David, it seems, didn't attempt to.

Finding a descendant of Jonathan wasn't easy. No one in David's circle knew one. Advisors summoned Ziba, a former servant of Saul. Did he know of a surviving member of Saul's household? Take a good look at Ziba's answer: "Yes, one of Jonathan's sons is still alive, but he is crippled" (2 Samuel 9:3 NLT).

Ziba mentions no name, just points out that the boy is lame. We sense a thinly veiled disclaimer in his words. "Be careful, David. He isn't—how would you say it?—suited for the palace. You might think twice about keeping this promise."

Ziba gives no details about the boy, but the fourth chapter of 2 Samuel does. The person in question is the firstborn son of Jonathan, Mephibosheth.

When Mephibosheth was five years old, his father and grandfather died at the hands of the Philistines. Knowing the brutality of the Philistines, the family of Saul headed for the hills. Mephibosheth's nurse snatched him up and ran, then tripped and dropped the boy, breaking both his ankles, leaving him incurably lame. Escaping servants carried him across the Jordan River to an inhospitable village called Lo Debar. The name means "without pasture." Picture a tumbleweed-tossed, low-rent trailer town in an Arizona desert. Mephibosheth hid there, first for fear of the Philistines, then for fear of David.

Collect the sad details of Mephibosheth's life:

- born rightful heir to the throne,
- victimized by a fall,
- left with halting feet in a foreign land,
- where he lived under the threat of death.

Victimized. Ostracized. Disabled. Uncultured.

"Are you sure?" Ziba's reply insinuates. "Are you sure you want the likes of this boy in your palace?"

David is sure.

Servants drive a stretch limousine across the Jordan River and knock on the door of a shack. They explain their business, load Mephibosheth into the car, and carry him into the palace. The boy assumes the worst. He enters the presence of David with the enthusiasm of a death-row inmate entering the lethal injection room.

The boy bows in great fear and asks,

> "Who am I that you pay attention to a stray dog like me?"
>
> David then called in Ziba, Saul's right-hand man, and told him, "Everything that belonged to Saul and his family, I've handed over to your master's grandson. . . . From now on [he] will take all his meals at my table." —9:8–10 MSG

Faster than you can say Mephibosheth twice, he gets promoted from Lo Debar to the king's table. Good-bye, obscurity. Hello, royalty and reality. Note: David could have sent money to Lo Debar. A lifelong annuity would have generously fulfilled his promise. But David gave Mephibosheth more than a pension; he gave him a place—a place at the royal table.

Look closely at the family portrait hanging over David's fireplace; you'll see the grinning graduate of Lo Debar High School. David sits enthroned in the center, flanked by far too many wives. Just in front of tanned and handsome Absalom, right next to the drop-dead beauty of Tamar, down the row from bookish Solomon, you'll see Mephibosheth, the grandson of Saul, the son of Jonathan, leaning on his crutches and smiling like he has just won the Jerusalem lottery.

Which indeed he had. The kid who had no legs to stand on has everything to live for. Why? Because he impressed David? Convinced David? Coerced David? No, Mephibosheth did nothing. A promise prompted David. The king is kind not because the boy is deserving, but because the promise is enduring.

For further proof, follow the life of Mephibosheth. He beds down in the bastion and disappears, temporarily, from Scripture for fifteen years or so.

◉ ◉ ◉

Disappearing was *not* an option, though Brad had briefly considered it that August day at the airport—when he got his first look at Cousin Theo.

It all began with a promise—and not just an ordinary promise, either. This one he'd made to his all-time-favorite aunt when she'd asked if he could help her son "land on his feet" in Brad's school when the whole family moved back to town. "No problem, Aunt Gia," he'd said instantly. "I'll take care of it."

She could have asked for the moon, and Brad would have agreed as readily. Of all his father's family, she was the one who most reminded him of his dad. Holiday dinners at Aunt Gia's laughter-filled table were one of Brad's favorite childhood memories. And when his fireman father's heroic act cost his life, Aunt Gia had been the rock Brad and his mom leaned on through the awful days that followed. He'd missed her a lot in the few years since that part of his family had moved to Texas. Now they'd be living here again! *What could possibly be better than that?*

Of course, that was before Cousin Theo flew in early to get a head start on his new life. Theo had changed so much since they'd last seen each other that Brad nearly walked right by his cousin in

144

baggage claim. What Brad was expecting was an older, more polished version of the brainy little guy with the gift for numbers, the knack for computers—and complete indifference to anything that didn't involve brainpower. What he got was a disaster.

It seemed Theo must have grown several inches *during* his flight. His rumpled cargo pants were way too short for his gangly legs. Every one of his multiple pockets was stuffed to over- flowing with the electronic gadgets he'd already retrieved from his suitcase. One of his . . . well . . . indescribable shoes was well on the way to finishing its full-course meal of a multicolored sock. And he topped it all off with a too-large wide-brimmed cowboy hat that kept slipping down his forehead to push his glasses askew. Somehow, Theo seemed to have raised nerdiness to an art form! In fact, he couldn't have done a better job had he planned it. *Wait a minute! Could it be that Theo plan—? Nah!*

"Hey, Brad . . . or as we say in Texas, 'Howdy, cousin!'" Theo's cheerful greeting snapped Brad most of the way out of his momentary trance.

"Uh . . . right back at you," was the best Brad could come up with.

The glint of humor in Theo's gray eyes—and his next comment—finished the job. "Kind of hopeless, huh, cuz?"

"No!" said Brad, although he suspected his expression had already given away his thoughts. But with a genuine hug for his cousin he said, "Just needs a little work." *Though how I'll pull this off, I have no idea!* "And there's plenty of time before school starts," he added, as much for himself as Theo. Surely he could come up with some way to help his disaster-of-a-cousin fit in at school. But what? Nice guy that Theo was—and he was!—Theo definitely wasn't in-crowd material.

Hold on! Where did that come from?! And why should it matter? That last thought opened a whole new can of worms for Brad. All of a sudden, he had *two* dilemmas to deal with: helping his cousin . . . and some very troubling thoughts about himself—what kind of person *he* was—that were starting to surface.

REBELLION

Fifteen years after his rescue by David, Mephibosheth resurfaces amid the drama of Absalom's rebellion.

Absalom, a rebellious curse of a kid, forces David to flee Jerusalem. The king escapes in disgrace with only a few faithful friends. Guess who is numbered among them. Mephibosheth? I thought you'd think so. But he isn't. Ziba is. Ziba tells David that Mephibosheth has sided with the enemy. The story progresses, and Absalom perishes and David returns to Jerusalem, where Mephibosheth gives the king another version of the story. He meets David wearing a ragged beard and dirty clothing. Ziba, he claims, abandoned him in Jerusalem and would not place him on a horse so he could travel.

Who's telling the truth? Ziba or Mephibosheth? One is lying. Which one? We don't know. We don't know because David never asks. He never asks because it didn't matter. If Mephibosheth tells the truth, he stays. If he lies, he stays. His place in the palace depends not on his behavior, but on David's promise.

Why? Why is David so loyal? And how? How is David so loyal? Mephibosheth brings nothing and takes much. From where does David quarry such resolve? Were we able to ask David how he fulfilled his giant-of-a-promise, he would take us from his story to God's story. God sets the standard for covenant-keeping.

As Moses told the Israelites:

> "Know this: GOD, your God, is God indeed, a God you can depend upon. He keeps his covenant of loyal love with those who love him and observe his commandments for a thousand generations."
> —Deuteronomy 7:9 MSG

God never breaks his promises. His irrevocable covenant runs like a scarlet thread through the tapestry of Scripture. Remember his promise to Noah?

> "I establish my covenant with you: Never again will all life be cut off by the waters of a flood; never again will there be a flood to destroy the earth." And God said, "This is the sign of the covenant I am making between me and you and every living creature with you, a covenant for all generations to come: I have set my rainbow in the clouds, and it will be the sign of the covenant between me and the earth." —Genesis 9:11–13 NIV

Every rainbow reminds us of God's covenant. Curiously, astronauts who've seen rainbows from outer space tell us they form a complete circle.[14] God's promises are equally unbroken and unending.

Abraham can tell you about promises. God told this patriarch that counting the stars and counting his descendants would be equal challenges. To secure the oath, God had Abraham cut several animals in half. To seal a covenant in the Ancient East, the promise-maker passed between a divided animal carcass, volunteering to meet the same fate if he broke his word.

> As the sun went down and it became dark, Abram saw a smoking firepot and a flaming torch pass between the halves of the carcasses. So the LORD made a covenant with Abram that day and said, "I have given this land to your descendants, all the way from the border of Egypt to the great Euphrates River." —Genesis 15:17–18 NLT

Need a picture of our promise-keeping God? Look at the smoldering pot passing between the animals. Look at the rainbow. Or look at Mephibosheth. You've never introduced yourself as Mephibosheth from Lo Debar, but you could. Remember the details of his disaster? He was

- born rightful heir to the throne,
- victimized by a fall, and
- left with halting feet in a foreign land,
- where he lived under the threat of death.

That's your story, too! Were you not born as a child of the King? Have you not been left hobbling because of the stumble of Adam and Eve? Who among us hasn't meandered along the dry sand of Lo Debar?

But then came the palace messenger. A fourth-grade teacher,

high-school buddy, an aunt, a television preacher. They came with big news and an awaiting limo. "You are not going to believe this," they announced, "but the king of Israel has a place for you at the table. The nameplate is printed and the chair is empty. He wants you in his family."

Why? Because of your IQ? God needs no counsel.

Your college fund? Not worth a dime to God.

Your organizational skills? Sure. The Architect of the universe needs your advice.

Sorry, your invitation has nothing to do with you and everything to do with God. He made a promise to give you eternal life. "God, who never lies, promised this eternal life before the world began" (Titus 1:2 GOD'S WORD).

Your eternal life is covenant-caused, covenant-secured, and covenant-based. You can put your Lo Debar in the rearview mirror for one reason—God keeps his promises. Shouldn't God's promise-keeping inspire yours?

⊙ ⊙ ⊙

Had it not been for his dad's inspiration, who knows *how* Brad would have dealt with the challenge presented by his way-less-than-cool cousin.

Brad, the promise-keeper—who'd always kept his word as effortlessly as he did everything else—was face-to-face with a commitment that could cost him a lot more to honor than just a little time and effort.

Brad, the confident denizen of the in-crowd—who rarely gave his own easy popularity a thought—now found himself wondering what it would be like not to be part of that elite scene. With Theo in tow, that was a very real possibility. As to why it should suddenly matter so much, Brad  had no more of a clue than . . . than Theo did about what to wear/say/do on almost any occasion. *And why am I being so judgmental about things that matter so little?!*

Still, Theo was family—another priority passed on to Brad by his dad—and, cool or not, a really good kid. He may not have a clue . . . but he did have feelings! *So love me, love my cousin. And let the chips fall where they may!*

That decided, Brad put his resourceful imagination to work and readjusted his priorities. Instead of helping Theo fit in, why not concentrate on helping him at least blend in! Three trips to the mall—and as many fruitless discussions about the relative merits of polos, crew-necks, and t-shirts—made it clear that Theo and style would never be friends.

They did have fun, though. Once Brad dragged him out of the electronics stores, Theo could be very good company indeed: a master of trivia, with a wry sense of humor, and the Morelli love of jokes, practical and otherwise. Despite Brad's best efforts, Theo still didn't look exactly stylish.

Fortunately, Theo also had the gift of being able to laugh at himself. "So Brad," he'd asked after their final mall excursion, "what happens if I don't become a fashion statement?"

Good question. But Brad's jangled nerves and jumbled emotions were busy elsewhere. First was his embarrassment about his cousin's lack of style and social smarts. Next came his guilt about being embarrassed, because he liked Theo. Brad was ashamed, too, that he might not be able to honor his promise to his aunt. Then all of that was pushed aside by the voice he remembered so well, the words he'd cherished and chosen to live by: "Easy or not, a promise is a promise. An honorable man keeps his word, son."

Clearly Brad needed another plan, and fast! Something that could change his friends' first reaction to Theo. Once they got to know him, they'd like Theo—but how could he get them to that point? *How can I get them to see the real Theo* inside *his uncool outside?* Brad repeated the question over and over in his mind. *How can I*—Suddenly, there it was: the answer. And a brilliant one, too: When you can't change reality, why not change perception! Politicians call it *spin*; Brad called it *looking on the bright side.*

By whatever name, it was a masterpiece of image-polishing that did no damage whatsoever to truth. It simply directed people past unimportant externals to the possibilities *inside.*

In the weeks before school started, everyone Brad talked to—which was everyone he could think of— heard about his *really interesting* cousin: the kid from Texas with the sharp wit and unique point of view who was . . . eccentric (not weird) . . . an original (not

151

clueless) . . . thoughtful (not dull) . . . and intriguing (not strange). But don't just take his word for it. They could see for themselves at Brad's backyard end-of-summer party.

As parties go, it was a huge success—mainly because of Theo's impromptu guitar/harmonica concert.

Brad had had his doubts when Theo—eyes glinting with Morelli mischief—offered to provide the entertainment. "Since I'm the star of this show, shouldn't I at least *perform*?" he'd asked with treacherous innocence. "I do play a couple of instruments, you know. And pretty well." That settled it. *Why not? Musical talent is always impressive.*

Brad assumed it would be some odd electronic musical instrument. What he got was an old-style twelve-string guitar and a harmonica. Theo's nimble fingers danced across the guitar strings, while he simultaneously began playing the harmonica. Even more amazing was his repertoire. Theo could play almost any song anyone asked for—and sing it, too. No doubt about it, Theo was a hit! One look at the crowd of laughing, chattering new friends who surrounded him whenever he took a break made that perfectly clear.

As Theo was rolling into an afternoon of encores, Aunt Gia—who'd flown in for the party—slipped her arm around Brad's shoulder. "You are so much like your dad," she said with a hug. "The way Tony always honored his word changed a lot of lives, just like you did Theo's today."

Tough Promises

When it comes to keeping promises, heaven knows you could use some inspiration. People can exhaust you. And there are times when all we can do is not enough. When a friend chooses to leave, we cannot force him or her to stay. When a friend abuses, we shouldn't stay. The best of love can go unrequited. I don't for a moment intend to minimize the challenges some of you face. You're tired. You're angry. You're disappointed. This isn't the problem you expected or the life you wanted. But looming in your past is a promise you made. May I urge you to do all you can to keep it? To give it one more try?

Why should you? So you can understand the depth of God's love.

When you love the unloving, you get a glimpse of what God does for you. When you keep the porch light on for the prodigal friend, when you do what is right even though you have been done wrong, when you love the weak, you do what God does every single moment. Covenant-keeping enrolls you in the postgraduate school of God's love.

Is this why God has given you this challenge? When you love liars, cheaters, and heartbreakers, are you not doing what God has done for us? Pay attention to and take notes on your struggles. God invites you to understand his love.

153

He also wants you to illustrate it.

David did with Mephibosheth. David was a walking parable of God's loyalty. He wardrobed divine devotion. My mother did for my father. I remember watching her care for him in his final months. ALS had sucked life from every muscle in his body. She did for him what mothers do for infants. She bathed, fed, and dressed him. She placed a hospital bed in the den of our house and made him her mission. If she complained, I never heard it. If she frowned, I never saw it. What I heard and saw was a covenant-keeper. "This is what love does," her actions announced as she powdered his body, shaved his face, and washed his sheets. She modeled the power of a promise kept.

God calls on you to do the same. Illustrate stubborn love. Incarnate fidelity. God is giving you a Mephibosheth-sized chance to show the world what real love does.

Embrace it. Who knows? Someone may tell your story of loyalty to illustrate the loyalty of God.

One final thought. Remember the family portrait in David's palace? I doubt if David had one. But I think heaven might. Won't it be great to see your face in the picture? Sharing the frame with folks like Moses and Martha, Peter and Paul . . . there will be you and Mephibosheth.

He won't be the only one grinning.

THIN AIR-OGANCE

CHAPTER 12

You can climb too high for your own good. It's possible to ascend too far, stand too tall, and elevate too much.

Linger too long at high altitudes, and two of your senses suffer. Your hearing dulls. It's hard to hear people when you are higher than they are. Voices grow distant. Sentences seem muffled. And when you are up there, your eyesight dims. It's hard to focus on people when you are so far above them. They appear so small. Little figures with no faces. You can hardly distinguish one from the other. They all look alike.

You don't hear them. You don't see them. You are above them.

Which is exactly where David is. He has never been higher. The wave of his success crests at age fifty. Israel is expanding. The country is prospering. In two decades on the throne, he has distinguished himself as a warrior, musician, statesman, and king. His cabinet is strong, and his boundaries stretch for sixty thousand square miles.

No defeats on the battlefield. No blemishes on his administration. Loved by the people. Served by the soldiers. Followed by the crowds. David is at an all-time high.

Quite a contrast with how we first found him in the Valley of Elah: kneeling at the brook, searching for five smooth stones. All others stood. The soldiers stood. Goliath stood. The others were high; David was low, belly down in the lowest part of the valley. Never lower, yet never stronger.

Three decades later his situation is reversed. Never higher, yet never weaker. David stands at the highest point of his life, in the highest position in the kingdom, at the highest place in the city—on the balcony overlooking Jerusalem.

He should be with his men, at battle, astride his steed and against his foe. But he isn't. He is at home.

> In the spring, when the kings normally went out to war, David sent out Joab, his servants, and all the Israelites. They destroyed the Ammonites and attacked the city of Rabbah. But David stayed in Jerusalem. —2 Samuel 11:1 NCV

It's springtime in Israel. The nights are warm, and the air is sweet. David has time on his hands, love on his mind, and people at his disposal.

Thin Air-ogance

◉ ◉ ◉

Life was sweet for Whitney Sanders. A double-chocolate supreme delight. With whipped cream. And a cherry on top. (And it's not even fattening!) What else would you expect? This is *Whitney* we're talking about here! And that was just the way things were—and always had been—in Whitney's on-top-of-the-world life. Extraordinarily pretty, remarkably talented, loaded with charm *and* intelligence, she'd been the center of attention practically from the cradle.

Whitney seemed to move effortlessly through life, surrounded by joy, laughter, and success. She could rise to any occasion, and met every expectation with confident ease and disarming humor. Anything she tried, she'd succeed at brilliantly. Anything she wanted just seemed to fall into her hands. But nobody seemed to mind. How could they? Just being around Whitney made *them* feel special, too, so they were happy to follow her lead in everything—what to wear, where to go, what to do.

And Whitney was happy to lead. If people wanted to come along while she went her merry way, what could possibly be wrong with that? Not a lot. Unless she took it all too much for granted. Or started to believe that success really *was* her birthright. Or forgot that when you're riding high, it's a long, long way to the ground. But she was way too smart to make that kind of mistake. Or was she?

With his army in the field and his conscience on hold, David stands on the balcony overlooking Jerusalem. His eyes fall upon a woman as she bathes. We'll always wonder if Bathsheba was bathing in a place where she shouldn't bathe, hoping David would look where he shouldn't look. We'll never know. But we know that he looks and likes what he sees. So he inquires about her. A servant returns with this information: "That woman is Bathsheba daughter of Eliam. She is the wife of Uriah the Hittite" (2 Samuel 11:3 NCV).

The servant laces his information with a warning. He gives not only the woman's name, but her marital status and the name of her husband, too. Why tell David she was married, if not to caution him? And why give the husband's name, unless David is familiar with it?

Odds are, David knew Uriah. The servant hopes to deftly dissuade the king. But David misses the hint. The next verse describes his first step down a greasy slope. "So David sent messengers to bring Bathsheba to him. When she came to him, he had sexual relations with her" (11:4 NCV).

David "sends" many times in this story. He *sends* Joab to battle (11:1). He *sends* the servant to inquire about Bathsheba (11:3). He *sends* for Bathsheba to have her come to him (11:4). When David later learns she is pregnant, he *sends*  word to Joab (11:6) to send Uriah back to Jerusalem. David *sends* him to Bathsheba to rest, but Uriah is too noble. David then opts to

send Uriah back to a place in the battle where he is sure to be killed. Thinking his cover-up is complete, David *sends* for Bathsheba and marries her (11:27).

We don't like this sending, demanding David. We prefer the pastoring David, caring for the flock; the dashing David, hiding from Saul; the worshiping David, penning psalms. We aren't prepared for the David who has lost control of his self-control, who sins as he sends.

◉ ◉ ◉

Whitney wasn't at all prepared when the *unexpected* dropped in, out of the blue, to tangle the threads of her always-smooth-as-silk life. But then, who—with the possible exception of Chicken Little—*ever* expects the sky to fall? Or has any idea what to do when it does?

But there it was—there *she* was—something Whitney had never before encountered in seventeen glorious, center-stage years: competition.

....

Blair Montgomery arrived on the scene without fanfare, thunderclap, or bells and whistles. But the effect was pretty much the same. From one week to the next, Monroe High had not one, but *two*, divas-in-residence.

Whitney's blue-eyed, blonde perfection was no less dazzling; but there was also a lot to be said for the drama of silver-gray eyes and shining, dark hair. Whitney's lively sense of fun and flashing smile could still light up a room; it was Blair's quirky point of view and dry wit that would have that same room in stitches. Whitney's soaring soprano, in choir or concert, could still stop hearts; but no more often, now, than Blair's velvety contralto voice.

And that was just the tip of the iceberg. From fashion to fun, from ridiculous to sublime, people who had always just naturally followed Whitney's lead now heard the intriguing beat of a different drummer. And—much to Whitney's astonished displeasure—followed it.

It needn't have been a contest at all. Blair and Whitney might have been friends. Indeed, they should have been. They had so much in common—startling good looks, amazing talent, and engaging charm. But charm can only carry you so far, as Whitney discovered—the day she looked behind her, and no one was following!

Someone else in her leadership role? Someone else starting trends? Someone else being looked to for cues on just about everything—what to wear, where to go, what to do? It just wasn't . . . right!

Whitney didn't exactly arch her back and hiss at the mere sight of Blair, but the claws certainly came out. It began with sniping . . . pointing out faults in Blair that no one else seemed to notice. From there it was just a short step to turning a sharp tongue on her friends as well. Her lighthearted chatter became more sarcastic than amusing; her temper, unpredictable; and her kindness, less so.

She might have been given a pass on some of it, but even for good friends, enough is enough. Could this . . . *stranger* . . . be their Whitney? And had they been wrong about her all along?

Whitney was not so sure herself.

ALTITUDE SICKNESS

What has happened to David to change him so completely? Simple. Altitude sickness. He's been too high too long. The thin air has messed with his senses. He can't hear like he used to. He can't hear the warnings of the servant or the voice of his conscience. Nor can he hear his Lord. The heights have dulled his ears and blinded his eyes. Did David see Bathsheba? No. He saw Bathsheba's body and Bathsheba's curves. He saw Bathsheba the conquest. But did he see Bathsheba the human being? The wife of Uriah? The daughter of Israel? The creation of God? No. David had lost his vision. Too long at the top will do that to you. Too many hours in the bright sun and thin air leaves you breathless and dizzy.

Of course, who among us could ever ascend as high as David? Who among us is a finger snap away from anything we want? Presidents and kings might send people to do their bidding; we're lucky to send out for pizza. We don't have that kind of clout.

We can understand David's other struggles. His fear of Saul. Long stretches hiding in the wilderness. We've been there. But David, high and mighty? David's balcony is one place we've never been.

Or have we?

I wasn't on a balcony, but I was on a flight. And I didn't watch a woman bathe, but I did watch an airline attendant fumble. She couldn't do anything right. Order soda, and she'd bring juice. Ask for a pillow, and she'd bring a blanket, if she brought anything at all.

And I started to grumble. Not out loud, but in my thoughts. *What's the matter with service these days?* I suppose I was feeling a bit smug. I'd just been a guest speaker at an event. People told me how lucky they were that I had come. I don't know what was loonier: the fact that they said it or that I believed it. So, I boarded the plane feeling cocky. I had to tilt my head to enter the doorway. I took my seat knowing the flight was safe, since, heaven knows, I'm essential to the work of God.

Then I asked for the soda, the pillow . . . she blew the assignments, and I growled. Do you see what I was doing? Placing myself higher than the airline attendant. In the pecking order of the plane, she was below me. Her job was to serve, and my job was to be served.

Now don't look at me like that. Haven't you felt a bit superior to someone? The waiter in a restaurant. A clerk at the mall. That new kid at school. You've done what I did. And we've done what David did. We've lost our sight and hearing.

When I looked at the airline attendant, I didn't see a human being; I saw a necessary commodity. But her question changed all that.

"Mr. Lucado?" Imagine my surprise when the airline attendant knelt beside my seat. "Are you the one who writes the Christian books?"

Thin Air-ogance

Christian books, yes. Christian thoughts, that's another matter, I said to myself, descending the balcony stairs. "May I talk to you?" she asked. Her eyes misted, and her heart opened, and she filled the next three or four minutes with her pain. Divorce papers had arrived that morning. Her husband wouldn't return her calls. She didn't know where she was going to live. She could hardly focus on work. Would I pray for her?

I did. But both God and I knew she was not the only one needing prayer.

Perhaps you could use a prayer, too. How is your hearing? Do you hear the servants whom God sends? Do you hear the conscience that God stirs?

And your vision? Do you still see people? Or do you see only their functions? Do you see people who need you, or do you see people beneath you?

● ● ●

Life looks a lot different from the cheap seats. And that's exactly where Whitney—who had always taken her first-class ticket through life for granted—ended up. And she had no one to thank for that but *herself*!

Oh, it did take a while for that fundamental truth to sink in. It was certainly more convenient—even grimly comforting—to blame that sneaky newcomer, Blair Montgomery, for "stealing" her rightful place as acknowledged leader in everything from fashion to fun. And, oh, did she miss that privileged status—and admiring friends—that had been her exclusive property for so long! *It's just not fair! How could this have happened to ME!?*

Whitney hadn't lost everything, of course. Somewhere deep inside, beneath the layers of anger, disappointment, and stunned disbelief, the caring and sensible Whitney was still alive and well—jumping and shouting and tugging at her sleeve.

> ANGER
> DISAPPOINTMENT
> DISBELIEF

Over the years, a lot of words—mainly superlatives—had been used to describe Whitney, but "arrogant" had never been one of them. Now it was—and Whitney was ashamed to admit it was true.

She'd been given all the golden gifts: looks, talent, friends. And at one time, she did appreciate her blessings and everyone around her. But somewhere along the line, riding way too high—Whitney caught a bad case of "altitude sickness" that caused her to stumble. She stopped seeing value in others. *At that point, she tumbled into a free fall.* She replaced "thank you" with "more." She stopped asking people to do things, and started ordering them.

As the too prideful often do, Whitney crashed hard. That's when she realized what she had done: She had been treating others as if they were just *accessories* that went with her popularity, rather than people . . . with feelings! *And they deserved so much better from me!* Even Blair Montgomery—challenge that she was to Whitney's one-of-a-kind status—was entitled to a gracious welcome to her new school.

Ashamed and embarrassed, Whitney knew she needed to get her priorities straight and make amends. *But how?* It wasn't going to be easy, but she knew with God's help she could find a way. And she did.

Whitney discovered she actually enjoyed being at eye level with people, rather than alone on the top of a mountain. She began showing her appreciation of others' talents by shifting the spotlight from herself to them. And when Blair Montgomery joined the drill team, it was Whitney who helped elect her team captain.

As Whitney learned to speak more softly and make requests rather than demands, her friends who'd missed her as much as she'd missed them began calling again. And, oh, was she glad they did. Because now Whitney knew something she'd never imagined in the rarified air of the heights: being "one of the crowd" wasn't a comedown; it was the warmest, most comforting place of all!

STORY OF POWER

The story of David and Bathsheba is less a story of lust and more a story of power. A story of a man who rose too high for his own good. A man who needed to hear the words "Come down before you fall."

"First pride, then the crash—the bigger the ego, the harder the fall" (Proverbs 16:18 MSG).

This must be why God hates arrogance. He hates to see his children fall. He hates to see his Davids seduce and his Bathshebas be victimized. God hates what pride does to his children. He doesn't dislike arrogance. He hates it. Could he state it any clearer than Proverbs 8:13: "I hate pride and arrogance" (NIV)? And then a few chapters later: "GOD can't stomach arrogance or pretense; believe me, he'll put those upstarts in their place" (Proverbs 16:5 MSG).

You don't want God to do that. Just ask David. He never quite recovered from his bout with this giant. Don't make his mistake. 'Tis far wiser to descend the mountain than to fall from it.

Pursue humility. Humility doesn't mean you think less of yourself, but that you think of yourself less. "Don't cherish exaggerated ideas of yourself or your importance, but try to have a sane estimate of your capabilities by the light of the faith that God has given to you" (Romans 12:3 PHILLIPS).

Embrace your poverty. We're all equally broke and blessed. "People come into this world with nothing, and when they die they leave with nothing" (Ecclesiastes 5:15 NCV).

Resist the place of celebrity. "Go sit in a seat that is not important. When the host comes to you, he may say, 'Friend, move up here to a more important place.' Then all the other guests will respect you'" (Luke 14:10 NCV).

Wouldn't you rather be invited up than put down?

God has a cure for the high and mighty—come down from the mountain. You'll be amazed by what you hear and whom you see. And you'll breathe a whole lot easier.

COLOSSAL COLLAPSES

CHAPTER 13

If a boxed set of DVDs existed documenting every second of your life, which parts would you erase? A folly-filled summer, a month off-track, days gone wild? Do you have a season in which you lost sight of what was right and thought only about what pleased you? Most of us have one, or more, of those.

King David did. Could a collapse be more colossal than his? He seduces and impregnates Bathsheba, murders her husband, and deceives his general and soldiers. Then he marries her. She bears his child.

The cover-up appears complete. The casual observer detects no cause for concern. David has a new wife and a happy life. All seems well on the throne. But all is not well in David's heart. Guilt simmers. He will later describe this season of secret sin in graphic terms:

When I kept it all inside, my bones turned to powder, my words became daylong groans. The pressure never let up; all the juices of my life dried up. —Psalm 32:3–4 MSG

David's soul resembles a Canadian elm in winter. Barren. Fruitless. Gray-shrouded. His harp hangs unstrung. His hope hibernates. The guy is a walking wreck. His season of folly stalks him like a pack of wolves. He can't escape it. Why? Because God keeps bringing it up.

Underline the last verse of 2 Samuel, chapter 11: "The thing that David had done displeased the LORD" (11:27). With these words the narrator introduces a new character into the David-and-Bathsheba drama: God. Thus far, he's been absent from the text, unmentioned in the story.

David seduces—no mention of God. David plots—no mention of God. Uriah buried, Bathsheba married—no mention of God. God is not spoken to and does not speak. The first half of verse 27 lures the reader into a faux happy ending: "[Bathsheba] became David's wife and gave birth to his son" (NCV). They decorate the nursery and pick names out of a magazine. Nine months pass. A son is born. And we conclude: David dodged a bullet. Angels dropped this story into the file marked "Boys will be boys." God turned a blind eye. Yet just when we think so and David hopes so . . . someone steps from behind the curtains and takes center stage. "The thing that David had done displeased the LORD."

God will be silent no more. The name not mentioned in chapter 11 dominates chapter 12. David, the "sender," sits while God takes control.

Colossal Collapses

⊙ ⊙ ⊙

Through all his precise planning and flawless follow-through, *one* thing had not occurred to Evan Forrest: When the wheels come off, even the most brilliant strategy can spin wildly out of control.

When Evan transferred to Ridgefield High a spring ago, he had put a lot of time, and imagination, into reinventing himself. Gone was the tough, street-smart kid who'd been in and out of trouble through much of elementary and middle schools on the other side of town. In his place was a smooth, sophisticated teen who took his cues from Hollywood's best. His disadvantaged childhood became a privileged one. His never-seen parents—the dad in prison, the mom who'd left long ago—were "traveling in Europe." The foster parents he was stuck with became an aunt and uncle he was staying with "just for a while."

It was beautiful fiction, told with absolute conviction and a master storyteller's flair for drama and detail. And it was so convincing that Evan himself started believing it.

How *did* a kid from the mean streets pull off a transformation so amazing? Relentless research—countless movies and videos for the look, the manner, the engaging charm. A con artist's talent (thanks to his dad) for convincing anyone of anything—including that he had been places he'd never been and done things that he'd never done. And a gift for blending seamlessly into his environment that chameleons would envy.

When there *was* a momentary glitch in the early days—something he said or did or wore that raised eyebrows—Evan carried that off, too, with the casual confidence of a trendsetter. By the time sophomore year rolled around, the charming guy who "preferred to set his own style" was automatically included in everything fun, exciting—or important—that happened at Ridgefield High. Even the faculty and staff—who *did* know Evan's backstory—were impressed by this smart, resourceful, *driven* kid who just "wanted a chance at a better life."

That *was* true. Evan *did* want a better life. He'd just never quite defined to himself what he meant by that—or wondered if there might be more to actually having it than just pretending. Oh, he did a great imitation of the kind of guy who fit the life he wanted. But lately he'd started to have a troubling suspicion that the reality of such a life had to be a lot more than just skin-deep—and that it might actually have to be earned. And how on earth could he do that?

Never mind, he told himself confidently, *I'll think of something.* Meanwhile, he'd just enjoy what he had and worry about the rest of it later.

It's all worked so far. What could possibly go wrong?

FISH BAIT

David may have hoped his sin would go unnoticed, but that hope ends when God sends Nathan to him. Nathan is a prophet, a preacher, a White House chaplain of sorts. The man deserves a medal for going to the king. He knows what had happened to Uriah. David had killed an innocent soldier . . . what will he do with a confronting preacher?

Still, Nathan goes. Rather than declare the deed, he relates a story about a poor man with one sheep. David instantly connects. He shepherded flocks before he led people. He knows poverty. He's the youngest son of a family too poor to hire a shepherd. Nathan tells David how the poor shepherd loved this sheep—holding her in his own lap, feeding her from his own plate. She was all he had.

Enter, as the story goes, the rich jerk. A traveler stops by his mansion, so a feast is in order. Rather than slaughter a sheep from his own flock, the rich man sends his bodyguards to steal the poor man's animal. They Hummer onto his property, snatch the lamb, and fire up the barbecue.

As David listens, hair rises on his neck. He grips the arms of the throne. He renders a verdict without a trial: fish bait by nightfall. "The man who has done this shall surely die! And he shall restore fourfold for the lamb, because he did this thing and because he had no pity" (2 Samuel 12:5–6).

Oh, David. You never saw it coming, did you? You never saw Nathan erecting the gallows or throwing the rope over the beam. You never felt him tie your hands behind your back, lead you up the steps, and stand you squarely over the trapdoor. Only when he squeezed the noose around your neck did you gulp. Only when Nathan tightened the rope with four three-letter words:

"You are the man!" (12:7).

David's face pales; his Adam's apple bounces. A bead of

sweat forms on his forehead. He sinks back in his chair. He makes no defense. He utters no response. He has nothing to say. God, however, is just clearing his throat. Through Nathan he proclaims:

> "I made you king over Israel. I freed you from the fist of Saul. I gave you your master's daughter and other wives to have and to hold. I gave you both Israel and Judah. And if that hadn't been enough, I'd have gladly thrown in much more. So why have you treated the word of GOD with brazen contempt, doing this great evil? You murdered Uriah the Hittite, then took his wife as your wife. Worse, you killed him with an Ammonite sword!" —12:7–9 MSG

God's words reflect hurt, not hate; bewilderment, not belittlement. Your flock fills the hills, why rob? Beauty populates your palace, why take from someone else? Why would the wealthy steal? David has no excuse.

So God levies a sentence.

> "Now, therefore, the sword will never depart from your house, because you despised me and took the wife of Uriah the Hittite to be your own. This is what the LORD says: 'Out of your own household I am going to bring calamity upon you. Before your very eyes I will take your wives and give them to one who is close to you, and he will lie with your wives in broad daylight. You did it in secret, but I will do this thing in broad daylight before all Israel.'"
> —12:10–12 NIV

From this day forward, turmoil and tragedy mark David's family. Even the child of his adultery will die (12:18). He must. Surrounding nations now question the holiness of David's God.

David had soiled God's reputation, blemished God's honor. And God, who jealously guards his glory, punishes David's public sin in a public fashion. The infant perishes. The king of Israel discovers the harsh truth of Numbers 32:23: "You can be sure that your sin will track you down" (MSG).

◉ ◉ ◉

Evan Forrest, master of illusion, was riding high . . . living the good life . . . having it all . . . with nary a cloud on his horizon. Until the day Evan—and a group of his most talkative new friends—ran into his past at the mall.

"Eddie? Eddie Flynn? Man, haven't seen you since *juvie!* And what *have* you done to yourself?!" Evan's lies were out. He'd have to face the consequences he had ignored—or never thought of at all.

It was textbook culture shock. On one side: the privileged style-setters who'd accepted Evan as one of their own. On the other: the scruffy kids in gang colors whose boisterous high-fives made it clear that Evan was one of *their* own, too. Given time to come up with a suitable fiction, Evan/Eddie might have pulled it off. But his resourceful imagination was stuck in neutral—and the look on his face said it all. And it was all downhill from there.

Evan lost a lot more that day at the mall than just the approval of his peers and his new life. And that *more* was the toughest pill of all

173

to swallow. Yes, he'd lied his way into his new reality—but there were a lot of things that came along with that life that he'd never expected and had started to like a lot.

He'd discovered through the service projects he'd been involved with—because it was the "in" thing to do—that it actually felt good to help someone other than himself.

He'd been amazed to realize that his agile mind worked as well in the classroom as it did in fabricating elaborate deceptions. He'd even started toying with the idea of college . . . someday.

He'd felt strangely at home in the church he'd attended a few times just because it seemed that was something his new friends did.

And who doesn't like being admired and sought out, even if the warm hellos were for someone who was pure fiction.

But all that was out of reach for him now. He'd fallen too far. And he knew it. In Evan's world, chances of any kind rarely came along. Second chances, never. Evan had blown a lot more than just fleeting popularity. And he didn't have a prayer of fixing things! Or did he?

UNWANTED GUEST

Do your sins show up to tap you on the shoulder? Does something you did hound you? Infect you? Colossal collapses won't leave us alone. They surface like a boil on the skin.

My brother had one once. In his middle-school years he contracted a case of boils. Poisonous pus rose on the back of his neck, like a tiny Mount St. Helens. My mom, a nurse, knew what the boil needed—a good squeezing. Two thumbs every morning. The more she pressed, the more he screamed. But she wouldn't stop until the seed of the boil popped out.

Gee, Max, thanks for the beautiful image.

I'm sorry to be so graphic, but I need to press this point. You think my mom was tough . . . try the hands of God. Unconfessed sins sit on our hearts like festering boils, poisoning, expanding. And God, with gracious thumbs, applies the pressure:

"The way of the transgressor is hard" (Proverbs 13:15 ASV).

"Those who plow evil and sow trouble reap evil and trouble" (Job 4:8 MSG).

God takes your sleep, your peace. He takes your rest. Want to know why? Because he wants to take away your sin. Can a mom do nothing as toxins invade her child? Can God sit idly as sin poisons his? He will not rest until we do what David did: confess our fault. "Then David said to Nathan, 'I have sinned against the LORD.' Nathan replied, 'The LORD has taken away your sin. You are not going to die'" (2 Samuel 12:13 NIV).

Interesting. David sentenced the imaginary sheep-stealer to death. God is more merciful. He put away David's sin. Rather than cover it up, he lifted it up and put it away. "As far as the east is from the west, so far has he removed our transgressions from us. As a father has compassion on his children, so the LORD has compassion on those who fear him" (Psalm 103:12–13 NIV).

It took David a year. It took a surprise pregnancy, the death of a soldier, the persuasion of a preacher, the probing and pressing of

God, but David's hard heart finally softened and he confessed: "I have sinned against the LORD" (2 Samuel 12:13).

And God did with the sin what he does with yours and mine—he put it away. It's time for you to put your wrongs to rest. Assemble a meeting of three parties: you, God, and your memory. Place the mistake before the judgment seat of God. Let him condemn it, let him pardon it, and let him "put it away."

He will. And he'll see you through the worldly consequences you've earned, too. If you ask him to.

After his spectacular downfall, Evan Forrest was the talk of the school in ways he'd never planned—or wanted.

Some couldn't wait to spread the news, with "fake" and "phony" their words of choice. Some could understand his wanting a better life, but still were furious about being lied to. Some just laughed, shrugged, and moved on.

Only one reached out to help. "You may not know it, Evan," said Cody Blake, "but I had a fling with reinventing myself, too. So I'm not about to cast the first stone." Then Cody grinned. "But I do have one to pass along."

Evan stared, puzzled, at the shifting golden fire inside the smooth stone Cody's unexpected handshake had slipped into his palm.

"It's called tiger's-eye," Cody explained. "I keep it handy to remind me of a guy named David who started with nothing, ended up with everything, *and* had to deal with more than a few giants along the way."

"David?" Evan, treading water frantically, was still out of his depth. Then a glimmer, if not the light, dawned. "You mean Bibl—?"

"Exactly," Cody confirmed, "Bible David. And boy, does he have a story for you!"

Evan got the *full* story on David—along with some supportive new friends—over sodas and snacks at Cody's house. Evan and The David Five covered a lot of ground that afternoon: hobbies and interests. Downfalls and comebacks. And the fine art of giant-slaying—including ways Evan could salvage his reputation by, like David, letting God put away his sin.

With Connor, Margaret, Sarah, Kyle—and, of course—Cody cheering him on, Evan was ready to stand tall in a new life, this one built on a foundation of truth. He continued to volunteer, mentor elementary school students, and help deliver meals to those in need. Soon, even those who'd said he was a "fake" or a "phony" were giving him another chance. Best of all was the way Evan used his creative talents to entertain rather than deceive—with ink-on-paper fiction and at storytelling events.

DASHED HOPES

CHAPTER 14

"I had intended . . ."

The David who speaks the words is old. The hands that swung the sling hang limp. The feet that danced before the ark now shuffle. Though his eyes are still sharp, his hair is gray and skin sags beneath his beard.

"I had intended . . ."

A large throng listens. Courtiers, counselors, chamberlains, and caretakers. They've assembled at David's command. The king is tired. The time for his departure is near. They listen as he speaks.

"I had intended to build . . ."

Odd way to start a farewell speech. David mentions not what he did but what he wanted to do yet couldn't. "I had intended to build a permanent home for the ark of the covenant of the LORD and for the footstool of our God" (1 Chronicles 28:2 NASB).

A temple. David had wanted to build a temple. What he had

done for Israel, he wanted to do for the ark—protect it.
What he had done with Jerusalem, he wanted to do with
the temple—establish it. And who better than he to do so? Hadn't
he, literally, written the book on worship? Didn't he rescue the ark
of the covenant? The temple would have been his swan song, his
signature deed. David had expected to dedicate his final years to
building a shrine to God.

At least, that had been his intention. "I had intended to build a
permanent home for the ark of the covenant of the LORD and for the
footstool of our God. So I made preparations to build it" (28:2 NASB).

Preparations. Architects chosen. Builders selected. Blueprints
and plans, drawings and numbers. Temple columns sketched. Steps
designed.

"I had intended . . . I made preparations . . ."

Intentions. Preparations. But no temple. Why? Did David
grow discouraged? No. He stood willing. Were the people resistant?
Hardly. They gave generously. Were the resources scarce? Far from
it. David "supplied more bronze than could be weighed, and . . .
more cedar logs than could be counted" (22:3–4 NCV). Then what
happened?

A conjunction happened.

Conjunctions operate as the signal lights of sentences. Some, such as *and*, are green. Others, such as
however, are yellow. A few are red. Sledgehammer red.
They stop you. David got a red light.

"I had made preparations to build it. *But* God said to me, 'You shall
not build a house for My name because you are a man of war and

have shed blood. . . . Your son Solomon is the one who shall build My house and My courts.'"— 1 Chronicles 28:2–3, 6 NASB, emphasis Max's

David's bloodthirsty temperament cost him the temple privilege. All he could do was say:

I had intended . . .
I had made preparations . . .
But God . . .

◉ ◉ ◉

The Mia Szabo who erupted into Cassie Hamilton's life like a high-energy bolt out of the blue one quiet afternoon in the hospital wasn't at all the Mia she'd always *expected* to be.

If things had gone as it once seemed they would, that eighteen-year-old Mia should have been in class right about then—polishing her talent—at Juilliard (or some *other* elite school of music). The word most applied to Mia from almost the first time she picked up a violin was *prodigy*.

Her technical brilliance—especially in one so young—was astonishing, but it was what happened when the green-eyed sprite tossed back that wild tumble of dark curls, tucked violin beneath chin, and set bow to strings, that took the breath away. Mia didn't simply *perform*; she took her audience with her—right into the heart of the music. And no one who experienced it ever forgot it.

180

Dashed Hopes

Determined to be the best, Mia practiced, and practiced, and practiced—and her hard work paid off.

And joyfully Mia shared her gift with her teachers, her family, her friends, her church, and anyone who wanted to listen—and they stood in line to listen. There was no doubt what Mia would do in her life. She had intended . . . She had made preparations . . . But God . . .

Mia looked down at her swollen, stiff fingers and frowned. Things had not worked out the way she had intended, for when Mia was fourteen, one little thing stopped her career: juvenile rheumatoid arthritis. JRA, if you want to use its friendlier-than-it-really-is nickname. JRA. Pain-bringer. Joint-twister. Dream-shaker.

The music that saturated Mia's soul still called her name as insistently. The amazing talent that was her gift still burned as brightly. The joy of performing still lured as sweetly. But her once-skillful fingers could no longer move with grace and precision. End of career. But not, although she didn't know it then, the end of Mia!

MY PLANS

I had intended . . .
I had made preparations . . .
But God . . .

I'm thinking of some people who have uttered similar words. God had different plans than they did.

One man waited until his midthirties to marry. Resolved to select the right spouse, he prayerfully took his time. When he found her, they moved westward, bought a ranch, and began their life together. After three short years, she was killed in an accident.

I had intended . . .
I had made preparations . . .
But God . . .

A young couple turned a room into a nursery. They papered walls, refinished a baby crib, but then the wife miscarried.

I had intended . . .
I had made preparations . . .
But God . . .

Willem wanted to preach. By the age of twenty-five, he'd experienced enough life to know he was made for the ministry. He sold art, taught language, traded books; he could make a living, but it wasn't a life. His life was in the church. His passion was with the people.

So his passion took him to the coal fields of southern Belgium. There, in the spring of 1879, this Dutchman began to minister to the simple, hardworking miners of Borinage. Within weeks his passion was tested. A mining disaster trapped scores of villagers. Willem nursed the wounded and fed the hungry; he even scraped the slag heaps to give his people fuel.

Dashed Hopes

After the rubble was cleared and the dead were buried, the young preacher had earned a place in their hearts. The tiny church overflowed with people hungry for his simple message of love. Young Willem was doing what he'd always dreamed of doing.

But . . .

One day his superior came to visit. Willem's lifestyle shocked him. The young preacher wore an old soldier's coat. His trousers were cut from sacking, and he lived in a simple hut. Willem had given his salary to the people. The church official was unimpressed. "You look more pitiful than the people you came to teach," he said. Willem asked if Jesus wouldn't have done the same. The older man would have none of it. This was not the proper appearance for a minister. He dismissed Willem from the ministry.

The young man was devastated. **WWJD**

He only wanted to build a church. He only wanted to do something good. He only wanted to honor God. Why wouldn't God let him do this work?

I had intended . . .
I had made preparations . . .
But God . . .

◉ ◉ ◉

After her arthritis was diagnosed, the irrepressible, always-helpful Mia seemed to disappear into a dark abyss.

First came denial. *Arthritis? Me?! No way! Probably just too much practice.* But no amount of practice could account for joints that stiffened and once-flexible fingers that no longer answered to her will.

Anger and frustration had their day, too, as *Okay, so I've got it!* gave way to the struggles—successful and not—of physical therapy. But Mia tilted a stubborn chin and soldiered on. *There has to be some way through this mess. All I have to do is find it!*

It was when she finally examined, and then embraced, the possibility that maybe God had something else in mind for her, that peace arrived—and Mia was able to move forward into the light. And she did it Mia-style, all the way. If living in harmony with God's will meant she'd have to learn to play a new kind of music, she'd become a virtuoso at that, *too!* And she did.

It wasn't an easy path, but Mia took it—and along the way, she helped others climb out of the abyss and into the light, too.

ATTITUDE

Years after they first met, Mia and Cassie would still save time in their busy schedules for each other. Their keep-in-touch luncheons were the first thing on each's new calendar—as if either would forget.

"Things are great, though I do have to tune up my attitude from time to time," Mia told Cassie at one of their catch-up sessions, "just to be sure it's still God's song I'm playing."

"I think it always is," said Cassie. Then she added with a grin, "Although your version can sometimes be a little . . . startling."

"But it got your attention, didn't it?" came the oh-so-innocent response.

Dashed Hopes

"Yes, it did. That, and *these*," Cassie added, dropping a small bag of five smooth stones on the table.

"You still have them, after all these years?" Mia asked.

"Well, of course," said Cassie, "they were a gift from a friend. They clicked encouragement when I laced on my running shoes and returned to the track. I carried them to my college graduation, and they jingled in my pocket all through my internship in pediatric medicine to remind me of Bible David . . . and you."

Mia beamed. "I keep mine handy, too. The day I accepted the award for my work in physical and music therapy, I figured I was the only adult in the room with five rocks in her pocket."

"No, you weren't. Mine were clicking applause from my front-row seat."

To others that day, Mia and Cassie may have seemed like two ordinary friends laughing their way through lunch. But what they didn't know was that the joy on their faces was the reflection of how truly blessed they were in the gifts God had given them on their roads from darkness to light.

BUT GOD

What do you do with the "but God" moments in life? When God interrupts your good plans, how do you respond?

The man who lost his wife has not responded well. At this writing he indwells a fog bank of anger and bitterness. The young couple is coping better. They stay active in church and are prayerful about a child. And Willem? Now that's a story. But before I share it, what about David? When God changed David's plans, how did he reply? (You'll like this.)

He followed the "but God" with a "yet God."

"Yet, the LORD, the God of Israel, chose me from all the house of my father to be king over Israel forever. For He has chosen Judah to be a leader; and in the house of Judah, my father's house, and among the sons of my father He took pleasure in me to make me king over all Israel." —1 Chronicles 28:4 NASB

Reduce the paragraph to a phrase, and it reads, Who am I to complain? David had gone from runt to royalty; from herding sheep to leading armies; from sleeping in the pasture to living in the palace. When you are given an ice-cream sundae, you don't complain over a missing cherry.

David faced the behemoth of disappointment with "yet God." David trusted.

So did Willem. Not at first, mind you. Initially, he was hurt and angry. He lingered in the small village for weeks, not knowing where to turn. One afternoon, he noticed an old miner bending beneath an enormous weight of coal. Caught by the pain and poignancy of the moment, Willem began to sketch the weary figure. His first attempt was crude, but then he tried again. He didn't know it, but at that very moment, he had discovered his true calling.

Not the robe of clergy, but the frock of an artist.

Not the pulpit of a pastor, but the palette of a painter.

Not the ministry of words, but of images. The young man the

leader would not accept became the artist the world could not resist, Vincent Willem van Gogh.[15]

His "but God" became a "yet God."

Who's to say yours won't become the same?

TAKE GOLIATH DOWN!

CHAPTER 15

He competes for the bedside position, hoping to be the first voice you hear. He covets your waking thoughts, those early, pillow-born emotions. He awakes you with words of worry, stirs you with thoughts of stress. If you dread the day before you begin your day, mark it down: your giant has been by your bed.

And he's just getting warmed up. He breathes down your neck as you eat your breakfast, whispers in your ear as you walk out the door, shadows your steps, and sticks to your hip. He checks your calendar, reads your email, and talks more trash than players in an inner-city basketball league.

"You ain't got what it takes."

"You come from a long line of losers."

"Fold your cards and leave the table. You've been dealt a bad hand."

Take Goliath Down!

He's your giant, your goliath. Given half a chance, he'll turn your day into his Valley of Elah, taunting, teasing, boasting, and echoing claims from one hillside to the other. Remember how Goliath misbehaved? "For forty days, twice a day, morning and evening, the Philistine giant strutted in front of the Israelite army" (1 Samuel 17:16 NLT).

Goliaths still roam our world. Disaster. Discrimination. Danger. Deceit. Disgrace. Disease. Depression. Doubt. Supersized challenges still swagger and strut, still pilfer sleep and embezzle peace and liposuction joy. But they can't dominate you. You know how to deal with them. You face your giants by facing God first.

> **Focus on giants—you stumble.**
> **Focus on God—your giants tumble.**

You know what David knew, and you do what David did. You pick up five stones, and you make five decisions. Ever wonder why David took five stones into battle? Why not two or twenty? Rereading his story reveals five answers:

1. The stone of the past *PAST*

Goliath jogged David's memory. Elah was a déjà vu. While everyone else quivered, David remembered. God had given him strength to wrestle a lion and strong-arm a bear. Wouldn't he do the same with the giant?

> David said to Saul, "Your servant used to keep his father's sheep, and when a lion or a bear came and took a lamb out of the flock, I went out after it and struck it, and delivered the lamb from its mouth; and when it arose against me, I caught it by its beard, and

struck and killed it. Your servant has killed both lion and bear; and this uncircumcised Philistine will be like one of them, seeing he has defied the armies of the living God." —17:34–36

A good memory makes heroes. A bad memory makes wimps. Amnesia made a wimp out of me last week. My goliath awoke me at 4:00 a.m. with a woeful list of worries. Our church was attempting to raise money for a youth building, more money than we had ever raised in one effort.

The giant awoke me with ridicule. *You guys are crazy. You'll never collect that much money.* I couldn't argue. *The economy is down. People are stressed. We may not raise enough to buy one brick.* Goliath had me running for the trees.

But then I remembered David, the nine-to-two odds, the story of the lion and the bear. So I decided to do what David did: gaze at God's victories. I climbed out of bed, walked into the living room, turned on the lamp, pulled out my journal, and began making a list of lion- and bear-sized conquests.

In the five previous years, God had prompted:

- a businessman to donate several acres of land to the church;
- another church to buy our old building;
- members to give above the needs, enabling the church to be 80 percent debt-free.

"God has done this before," I whispered. A lion's head hangs in the church foyer and a bear rug rests on the sanctuary floor. About this time, I heard a thud. Right there in the living room! I turned around just in time to see Goliath's eyes cross and knees buckle and body fall face-first on the carpet. I stood and placed a foot on his back and chuckled. *Take that, big boy.*[16]

"Remember His marvelous works which He has done" (1 Chronicles 16:12). Catalog God's successes. Keep a list of his world records. Has he not walked you through high waters? Proven to be faithful? Have you not known his provision? How many nights have you gone to bed hungry? Mornings awakened too cold? He has made road kill out of your enemies. Write today's worries in sand. Chisel yesterday's victories in stone. Pick up the stone of the past, and put history on your side.

◉ ◉ ◉

What's in your past? Remember the things God has already done for you. Memories of his father helped **Brad Morelli** keep honor on the top of his "to-do" list. When things got tough, Brad replayed his father's words in his mind: "Easy or not, a promise is a promise. An honorable man keeps his word, son." And that irrepressible violin prodigy **Mia Szabo** discovered that the determination, work ethic, and positive attitude she had developed in perfecting her violin skills were even more powerful in her fight against juvenile rheumatoid arthritis.

Your goliath might be different, but the answer is the same. Follow David's fail-safe solution for any quandary by trusting God to help you build on your strengths.

DIFFERENT PLANS

With a firm grip on the stone of the past, now select:

2. The stone of prayer

Before going high, David went low; before ascending to fight, David descended to prepare. Don't face your giant without first doing the same. Dedicate time to prayer. Paul the apostle wrote: "Prayer is essential in this ongoing warfare. Pray hard and long" (Ephesians 6:18 MSG).

Prayer spawned David's successes. His Brook Besor wisdom grew out of the moment he "strengthened himself in the LORD his God" (1 Samuel 30:6). When Saul's soldiers tried to capture him, David turned toward God: "You have been my defense and refuge in the day of my trouble" (Psalm 59:16).

How do you survive a fugitive life in the caves? David did with prayers like this one: "Be good to me, God—and now! I've run to you for dear life. I'm hiding out under your wings until the hurricane blows over. I call out to High God, the God who holds me together" (Psalm 57:1–2 MSG).

When David soaked his mind in God, he stood. When he didn't, he flopped. You think he spent much time in prayer the evening he seduced Bathsheba? Did he write a psalm the day he murdered Uriah? Doubtful.

Mark well this promise: "[God] will keep in perfect peace all who trust in [God], whose thoughts are fixed on [God]!" (Isaiah 26:3 NLT). God promises not just peace, but perfect peace. Undiluted, unspotted, unhindered peace. To whom? To those whose minds are "fixed" on

God. Forget occasional glances. Dismiss random ponderings. Peace is promised to the one who fixes thoughts and desires on the King.

Invite God's help. Pick up the stone of prayer.

● ● ●

Do you make time for prayer in your life? **Cassie Hamilton** let anger, fear, and frustration hold her hostage after her accident—until she remembered to talk to God. **Jenna Gordon** shunned God after the death of her twin—until she realized that God had always been with her.

Do you have a goliath who is working to keep you from God? Remember that God is your powerhouse! Talk to him—anytime, anywhere, any day. He's still there ready to listen, whether prayer is something new for you or it's just been a while since you last talked to God.

PICK UP YOUR STONE

With the stones of the past and prayer securely in hand, now pick up:

3. The stone of priority PRIORITY

This third stone is a reminder of your highest priority: God's reputation. David jealously guarded it. No one was going to defame his Lord. David fought so that "all the earth may know that there is a God in Israel. Then all this assembly shall know that the

LORD does not save with sword and spear; for the battle is the LORD's"
(1 Samuel 17:46–47).

David saw Goliath as God's chance to show off! Did David know he would exit the battle alive? No. But he was willing to give his life for the reputation of God.

What if you saw your giant in the same manner? Rather than begrudge him, welcome him. Your cancer is God's chance to flex his healing muscles. Your sin is God's opportunity to showcase grace. Your struggles with "following the crowd" in ways that are foolish, dangerous, or hurtful to others can billboard God's power. See your struggle as God's canvas. On it he will paint his multicolored supremacy. Announce God's name, and use the stone of priority.

 ⦿ ⦿ ⦿

Where are your priorities? Are you a living example of the power of a God-centered approach to life like **Connor Ryan**, who was finally able to see himself *and* his archrival as "God's unfinished projects"? Or maybe you are a quiet world-changer like **Sam Mitchell**, who transforms many lives one simple, small kindness at a time. One simple act. Think about how Sam's priority of doing "the right thing" set in motion a ripple of kindness that turned into a tidal wave that **Suri Prabhakar** rode to the stars.

Whatever battle your goliath chooses, welcome the opportunity to let God claim a victory for you.

Take Goliath Down!

Armed with the stones of past, prayer, and priority, now you're ready for:

4. The stone of passion PASSION

> As Goliath moved closer to attack, David quickly ran out to meet him. Reaching into his shepherd's bag and taking out a stone, he hurled it from his sling and hit the Philistine in the forehead. The stone sank in, and Goliath stumbled and fell face downward to the ground. —17:48–49 NLT

David ran not away from, but toward, his giant. On one side of the battlefield, Saul and his cowardly army gulped. On the other, Goliath and his skull-splitters scoffed. In the middle, the shepherd boy ran on his spindly legs. Who bets on David? Who puts money on the kid from Bethlehem? Not the Philistines. Not the Hebrews. Not David's siblings or David's king. But God does.

And since God does, and since David knew God did, the skinny runt becomes a blur of pumping knees and a swirling sling. He runs toward his giant.

Do the same! What good has problem-pondering gotten you? You've stared so long you can number the hairs on Goliath's chest. Has it helped?

No. Listing hurts won't heal them. Itemizing problems won't solve them. Categorizing rejections won't remove them. David lobotomized the giant because he emphasized with the Lord. And did it with all his heart!

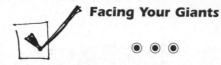

Facing Your Giants

● ● ●

What is your passion? Is it like **Cody Blake's** burning desire to find out, explore, and *know* just about everything about just about anything? Or more like **Cassie Hamilton's**, who discovered a passion for a race of quite another kind—one where it wasn't the number of legs that mattered, but the quality of the heart.

Is there a goliath stealing your passion? Reclaim it by emphasizing God.

ONE MORE STONE

With the stones of past, prayer, priority, and passion at your command, you may feel ready to lead on the six o'clock news. But wait . . . one more stone remains:

5. The stone of persistence PERSISTANCE

David didn't think one rock would do. He knew Goliath had four behemoth relatives. "Ishbi-benob was a descendant of the giants; his bronze spearhead weighed more than seven pounds" (2 Samuel 21:16 NLT). Saph made the list, described as "another descendant of the giants" (21:18 NLT). Then there was "the brother of Goliath of Gath. The handle of his spear was as thick as a weaver's beam!" (21:19 NLT). These three seem harmless compared to King Kong.

> There was a giant there [Gath] with six fingers on his hands and six toes on his feet—twenty-four fingers and toes! He was another of those descended from Rapha. . . . These four were descended from Rapha in Gath. —21:20, 22 MSG

Take Goliath Down!

Why did David quarry a quintet of stones? Could it be because Goliath had four brothers the size of Tyrannosaurus rex? For all David knew, they'd come running over the hill to defend their kin. David was ready to empty the chamber, if that's what it took.

Imitate him. Never give up. One prayer might not be enough. One apology might not do it. One day or month of resolve might not suffice. You may get knocked down a time or two . . . but don't quit. Keep loading the rocks. Keep swinging the sling.

● ● ●

So, how persistent *are* you? Are you like **Kyle Perry**, who, when he finally met an irresistible opportunity, put his multiple talents to work for others—sank in his teeth and stuck with it? Remember **Evan Forrest**, whose every lie about his past fed his goliath—until Evan faced the truth and its consequences and picked up the stone of persistence. It took a while, but by persistently demonstrating how he'd changed in multiple ways—being truthful, helping others, and attending church—Evan created a promising future.

Is there a goliath keeping you from your goals? Conquer him with persistence. Lean on God to help you keep doing your best, keep working your hardest, keep doing the right thing . . . keep trying.

REACH FOR A STONE

David took five stones. He made five decisions. Do likewise. Past. Prayer. Priority. Passion. And Persistence.

Next time Goliath shows up, reach for a stone. Odds are, he'll be out of the room before you can load your sling.

NOTES

1. Max Lucado's paraphrase.
2. Max Lucado's paraphrase.
3. http://www.oklahomacitynationalmemorial.org
4. M. Norville Young with Mary Hollingsworth, *Living Lights, Shining Stars: Ten Secrets to Becoming the Light of the World* (West Monroe, LA: Howard Publishing, 1997), 39.
5. Ernest Gordon, *To End All Wars: A True Story About the Will to Survive and the Courage to Forgive* (Grand Rapids: Zondervan, 2002), 105–6, 101.
6. Hans Wilhelm Hertzberg, *I and II Samuel*, trans. J. S. Bowden (Philadelphia: Westminster Press, 1964), 199–200.
7. Associated Press, "450 Sheep Jump to their Deaths in Turkey," July 8, 2005.
8. C. J. Mahaney, "Loving the Church," audiotape of message at Covenant Life Church, Gaithersburg, MD, n.d., quoted in Randy Alcorn, *Heaven* (Wheaton, IL: Tyndale House, 2004), xxii.
9. Eugene H. Peterson, *Leap Over a Wall: Earthy Spirituality for Everyday Christians* (San Francisco: HarperSanFrancisco, 1997), 65.
10. Isaiah 40:31 NIV.
11. Ann Kaiser Stearns, *Living Through Personal Crisis* (New York: Ballantine Books, 1984), 6.
12. George Arthur Butterick, ed., *The Interpreter's Dictionary of the Bible: An Illustrated Encyclopedia* (Nashville: Abingdon, 1962), s.v. "Urim and Thummin," and Merrill C. Tenney, gen. ed., *Pictorial Bible Dictionary* (Nashville: Southwestern Company, 1975), s.v. "Urim and Thummim."
13. F. B. Meyer, *David: Shepherd, Psalmist, King* (Fort Washington, PA: Christian Literature Crusade, 1977), 101–2.
14. Fred Lowery, *Covenant Marriage: Staying Together for Life* (West Monroe, LA: Howard Publishing, 2002), 44.
15. Paul Aurandt, *Paul Harvey's the Rest of the Story*, ed. and comp. Lynne Harvey (New York: Bantam Books, 1978), 107–9.
16. The offering exceeded our expectations.